VIRTUAL MAGIC

Amaze Your Friends With Fun Tricks
You Can Perform Online!

Cris Johnson

ElementarySchoolAssemblies.com

Virtual Magic: Amaze Your Friends with Fun Tricks You Can Perform Online.

Cris Johnson

ISBN#: 978-1-7356893-3-3

First Printing: October 2020

Portions of this book were originally incorporated into the curriculum of the Buffalo Magic Academy that teaches children fun magic tricks as well as critical social life skills

Cristopher J. Johnson

Cris Johnson, Inc.
8310 Lockport Rd.
Niagara Falls, NY 14304

(716) 940-8963

www.ElementarySchoolAssemblies.com

Cris Johnson is available to speak at your elementary or middle school on a variety of topics. Call (716) 940-8963 for booking information.

Why Read This Book

Confidence. Respect for others. Being prepared. Active listening. These skills and more are recognized as crucial skills in the social development of children.

By framing the magic effects in this book as being perfect for the internet, this book gives the reader fun tools to perform magic for family members and friends far away! On top of that, readers of this book will be able to get access to videos of each magic trick conducted and explained by the author.

With *Virtual Magic*, the sleights and secrets are easy to understand. This book is fun, engaging, and features a lot of emphasis not only on the performance of the tricks themselves but also key things to consider that will encourage young readers to become empathetic and compassionate performers. All of this is done in a way that flies "below the radar" so readers can absorb the material without losing sight of the point of magic, which is to have fun.

Whether learning how to float a dollar bill in the air, multiply money, or predict the future, this book serves as a fun introduction to an amazing art form.

Do you love science?

Cars, smart phones, televisions, ceiling fans, dishwashers, and on and on...none of it would be available to us without advances in science. Science is amazing by itself, but by combining superheroes and science, this book is an irresistible combination to young readers! Why?

Kids LOVE superheroes! By using simple science experiments that seem to reproduce superhero powers, kids will be hooked! On top of that, readers of this book will be able to get access to videos of each experiment conducted and explained by the author.

With *Super Science*, the lessons and concepts are easy to understand. This book is funny, silly, and features a lot of weird ways to illustrate scientific principles for young readers. From asking the question "Can a hot dog fly?" as a way to explain the Scientific Method to wondering "Did the President of The United States steal my bicycle?" to illustrate what makes a good hypothesis, and why dropping pizza on your sidewalk will help you understand Potential and Kinetic energy, this book is a wild, wacky way to learn fun science experiments that anyone can do safely.

**Get the new book to help put your kids
unleash their own superpowers!**

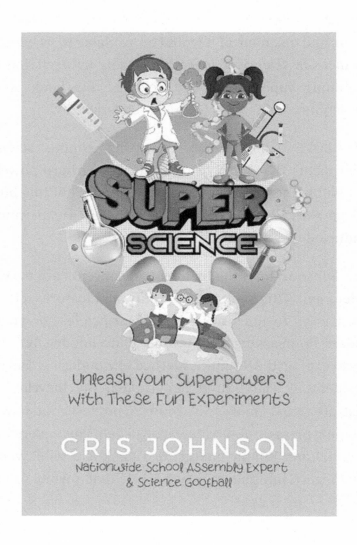

Written by a School Assembly Expert with 20 Years' Experience Holding the Attention of Children

Cris Johnson is an experienced school assembly presenter, having traveled across North America delivering programs. He performs 400 shows a year and offers over a dozen assembly topics including bully prevention, drug awareness, character education, reading, recycling, and many more.

Cris Johnson is also a Board-Certified Hypnotist & Instructor through the National Guild of Hypnotists and a Master Practitioner & Trainer of Neuro-Linguistic Programming, giving him unique insights into how people of all ages think and process information. Cris is an accomplished speaker on topics such as stress management, teambuilding in the workplace, communication strategies, and more.

Do you want Cris Johnson to be the motivational speaker at your next event?

Call (716) 940-8963 or visit

www.FunCorporateTeamBuilding.com

What others have to say about Cris Johnson's

educational live programs

"Cris Johnson is someone you most definitely want to come visit your school and present to your students! His professionalism, charisma, and programs are far above the rest. He handles every last detail himself and makes every part of bringing his assembly programs (from scheduling to day-of setup) easy for the principal and school. The caliber of his program content is perfect for students in today's ever changing and growing complex world. Whether he is showcasing character traits or test taking strategies, your students will be engaged and listening as a result of his mix of high interest tricks, media, and sensory inputs with choice language and explicit powerful messaging. By far what makes Cris the best assembly program provider for your school though is his ability to manage a large crowd! From the time the kids enter your gym, cafeteria, or multipurpose room to the time they reenter the classroom, Cris has them following his every lead in being respectful and courteous, quiet when necessary, and participating appropriately. Never have I had an assembly end so calmly and quiet!"

Kelly Moran, Ed.D., *Principal*

"These are just some of the things said by teachers, children and parents about Cris Johnson's performance. His magic show was unbelievable and left everyone amazed. His ability to integrate entertainment with an educational message was phenomenal. He kept full control of the children while allowing them to relax and enjoy the show. It is rare to find a character education show that not only delivers a powerful message to the children, but also entertains to this degree. This is definitely a show you want to have at your school!"

Mary Dettelis, *PTO*

"Cris is very energetic and funny. This kids and the teachers were very impressed. They LOVED it! We want to book Cris for next year already! One of our sixth grade teachers said it was the BEST assembly presented at this school in 20 years!"

Amy Mckenty, *School Librarian*

"Our school was fortunate enough to have Cris Johnson inform and entertain our whole school last week. I can assure you that you will not be disappointed in this presentation. He presented two shows; one to the primary and one to the intermediate grades. In doing this, he could adjust the show to the age levels. He captivated all of the children's attention throughout the entire show and truly knew how to control his audience throughout his magic acts. His greatest compliment came from a child in my room who commented as we were leaving the gym by saying, "I loved that guy!" The students are still using his advice. Any school would be lucky to have Cris come and present his Assembly!"

Bonnie Montana, *Second Grade Teacher*

"Thanks again for coming to Hill and Plain. It is so hard to find Character Education programs for our young students but your shows NEVER disappoint. Several teachers remarked how good you are and I love your messages: The message about not judging others from what they see but how you got to get to know the student and know them from the inside. Also the last magic trick about including others...that visual was so ON key. Having the white little block left out was so evident to the students and they comprehended well. I also loved the magic trick where the strong kid can't pick up the box...it was perfect for that particular kid because he's pretty popular and having him not be the "one" that succeeds was perfect."

Heliett Sanchez, *School Counselor*

"We were all very pleased with the show that you put on. Your messages and magic tricks were appropriate for all and played to all grade levels. I saw just as many fifth graders amazed by the magic and jumping out of their sitting positions to volunteer as I did kindergarten and first graders. Feedback from all grade levels was equally positive. We liked that the show was interactive and helped make the general audience, as well as specific students, a part of the performance. Furthermore, your messages and main themes were all clearly explained and to the point. Students came away from the performance understanding what it means to be a "HERO" and how they can help those being bullied or handle it if it happened to them. I can actually say I've used a few of the points you made since I saw the show (making sure to tell an adult, asking the other person to stop) in dealing with interactions and issues between students. Thank you for a quality performance and for bringing much happiness to our students that day and the days to follow."

Thomas Lanza, *Supervisor of Instruction*

Table of Contents

Chapter 1:
Introduction

Do you love magic?

I know I do—I have been performing magic for most of my life! When I was eight years old, my mom and dad gave me my first magic set, and I have been hooked on magic ever since!

In this book, you are going to learn some very special magic tricks—magic that is perfect for performing for your friends or relatives over the internet using Zoom or other video platforms.

A lot of the magic tricks that exist might not be the best for the Internet because you would need someone to pick a card, hold onto an object, or write something down. With these tricks, your friends can just watch and enjoy the magic without having to touch anything.

This type of magic is perfect if you live really far away from someone and you want to show them magic. But it wasn't always possible to do magic in this way. Things have really changed since I first became interested in magic!

Of course, if you are reading this book and wondering, "who is this dude and why should I pay attention to what he says about magic?" Let me explain why I can talk about magic and help you become an awesome internet magician superstar.

For the last 20 years, I have been a full-time professional magician, meaning that's how I earn money to pay for my house, car, and dog food (the dog food is not for me, it's for my dogs).

During most of those 20 years, most of the magic I have done has been for schools, probably like yours. If your school doesn't have school assemblies, here's what I mean by doing magic for schools: I am hired by someone at the school to come and talk to the students about something really important, such as why people should not bully each other, or why it's important to try your hardest.

Here's the deal: if I just came to your school and started telling you what to do, you would probably get really bored really fast and stop listening to what I'm saying. So,

I use fun magic to help explain what I'm talking about keep everyone interested in what I have to say!

I perform about 400 shows a year in schools and libraries, and speak in front of audiences of 400, 500, or even 600 kids at a time!

So I really know magic!

In this book, you are not only going to learn really cool magic for the internet, but I will also tell you really cool stuff to think about so your magic is more interesting to people you show it to.

Of course, some people reading this book might want to ask me, "Hey, magic dude, why are you doing a book on magic with tricks for the internet?"

Great question! I'm glad you asked. I'm writing this book because our world is getting smaller!

Okay, don't go running outside to see if all kinds of things are shrinking, because it's not... at least not while I'm writing this book!

Saying the 'world is getting smaller' means that because of the internet and other technology, keeping in touch with someone really far away is much easier now than it used to be. Let's say your grandma lives in California and you live in New York. You can call her on the phone, text her, Facetime her, see her on Zoom, and all kinds of other ways.

Back when I was a kid, if my grandma was really far away, I could write her a letter and mail it, and it would take days to get there. Or I could call her on the phone, but I still couldn't see her face.

The internet has changed everything. It's the same with performing magic—when I first started performing magic professionally, the only way to see my magic live was to go to the building where I was performing and watch my show live. But now? Because of Zoom and other cool things, I can do magic for people anywhere in the world!

I can also teach magic to anyone anywhere in the world too! In fact, I even now have my own Magic School where I teach kids magic with special tricks they get in the mail. I'll talk more about my school later.

So that's why I'm writing this book—to celebrate how the internet allows magicians to perform magic now for anyone in the world!

Here's another reason why I wrote this magic book...when I was very young, most of the magic books did not give you very much detail about the trick. In some books, there would be just a few sentences explaining how each trick worked. Other books would have just a little drawing showing the secret.

In magic, the 'secret' is just one part of being able to perform magic and amaze people. There are a lot of little details to think about. So when I explain how the tricks work, I'm going to give a lot of details to help you really understand the trick. And in this book, you will learn so much more than just tricks.

You'll also learn ways to keep people interested in what you are saying when you perform magic, ways to make your magic more fun, things to think about so you have more fun performing it, and so much more!

I organized this book by chapters—each chapter has three tricks in it. Each chapter teaches tricks in a certain category. There's a chapter on magic with string, a chapter on tricks with money, a chapter on tricks with playing cards, and lots more! I arranged every chapter like this so it would be easier for you to look up a certain trick later, after you have read the whole book.

Here's the deal—in every category of magic (card tricks, coin tricks, rope tricks, and on and on) there are like six BILLION different kinds of magic tricks, so six billion card tricks, six billion coin tricks... well, you get the idea.

That means when I was picking tricks for this book, I had a lot of magic to look through and decide if each trick would look good on the internet, if it would fool people, and if each trick did not need your audience to have to touch or hold anything.

Since each chapter has three tricks, I included a really easy trick, a medium-level trick, and finally a trick that takes a little more work. For the tricks that are more challenging, maybe that means the trick uses more sleight of hand, or sometimes, the more challenging tricks in a chapter might need a little arts-and-crafts work on your part—maybe there's things to glue, tape, or cut.

By the way, if you are brand new to magic, 'sleight of hand' means using your hands in sneaky ways to make the trick look like magic.

None of the tricks in this book are really hard, but I wanted to include tricks of different skill levels so if you are just starting out, you can learn a really easy trick, and after you have mastered that trick, then you can move on to one of the more challenging tricks.

In some cases, when I write about how to do the trick, I will use a lot of words to describe something that is very easy to do. But sometimes, it is just easier to see it. Many magic books include drawings to help their readers understand what to do. I did not include drawings in this book because I am not very good at drawing. A lot of magic books that I read growing up had pretty poor drawings in them. I would look at the drawings, and when I had trouble understanding what I was supposed to do, I would feel very frustrated.

For that reason, instead of including bad drawings, each trick in this book comes with a video of me performing and explaining the trick.

Watching me do the trick on a webpage makes learning magic easier, but here's something really important to think about: Reading the words in a book and working to understand them exercises your brain, which makes you smarter. When your brain gets used to working like that, you'll understand how to do magic faster and easier.

What this means is—don't just go to the videos right away. Try using just my words in this book to understand what to do first, and then watch the videos later to see if you got everything right.

Before we get to the really awesome magic, I have included something very special in this book. The next two chapters are filled with ideas and tips (and even some rules) of magic that can help you not only do great magic that will amaze people, but also ways to make sure the people watching your tricks are having a really good time.

I have to also tell you something really scary.

When I was very young, I learned most of my magic by reading books just like this one. Back when I was a kid, we didn't have very many ways to watch videos of magic—no video tapes, no DVDs, no Bluerays. We did not even have the internet to watch videos.

Okay, I'm going to pause for a moment because I'll bet some of you reading this are totally freaking out because we didn't have the internet when I was your age.

So, go ahead and freak out...

All done? Yup, no internet when I was a kid, so you know what that means?

I'm old. Yup.

Getting so old I might get forgetful and have trouble remembering what book I'm writing.

Hmmm, what am I writing about? Broccoli? Okay!

So, if you are ready to learn all about broccoli, raise your hands in the air and start cheering!

I'm just kidding... this is NOT a book about broccoli!

All right, back to the videos... like I said, I learned most of my magic when I was very young by reading books, and books are awesome, which is why I write books and why I read even more books.

Here's another reason why I wrote this book and also included videos: When it comes to learning things, scientists who study how people learn have realized that people learn the best when they are able to learn the same stuff in different ways. So maybe your teacher tells you something. Then maybe your teacher writes something on the board. Then later, you watch a video. It's all the same stuff, but your brain learns faster when the same information is presented different ways.

The way you will get to see the videos is very simple: At the end of each chapter, I will include a special website that your parents can take you to where you can see me perform every trick and then explain it.

Really, the website is going to be the same for every trick, but I will include the website at the end of every chapter so no matter where you are in the book, you will be able to find the website easily.

You are going to have to ask your mom or dad to go to the website for you, because while the internet is super fun, you also want to be super careful because there's a lot of weird stuff on the internet... like a Why Broccoli Is Awesome Website!

Okay, maybe not a broccoli website. But you will still want your mom or dad to go to the website for you.

In addition to the tricks, in the next two chapters I will do something that most magic books I read growing up did NOT do: I'm going to teach you some things that are even more important than the secrets to the tricks. If you do these things, your magic will be even MORE amazing, because magic is about so much more than just secrets.

And you know what? If you do the things that I talk about in the next two chapters, people will enjoy watching you perform magic because it will be YOU performing!

What all of this means is that by the end of this book, if you follow along and practice, not only will you learn some really awesome magic that you can show your friends over the internet, but you are going to learn some really important things that can help you in life, not just magic!

The next chapter will teach you the Top 10 Rules of Magic! This is probably the most important chapter in the book, so if you are ready to get started, turn the page!

Chapter 2:

The Top 10 Rules of Magic

Now we're getting into the really good stuff!

The things in this chapter will help you amaze people and hide the secrets of magic. You see, knowing the secret is only part of what makes magic special. People watching magic are smart, and people can figure things out.

That means that there are things that you can do while performing magic to help hide the secret and along the way, make magic more... well, magical! So, with that in mind...

Here are my Top 10 Rules of Magic...

Rule #1 - Practice your magic before you show anyone!

This is the biggest reason why some people figure magic tricks out. The magician performing the tricks has not practiced enough so the moves are not smooth.

I can understand why some magicians show a trick before they have practiced. Maybe the way the trick works is so easy that the magician thinks, "Oh, there's no way anyone will figure this out. And it's so easy, I can show my friends right away!"

Even though a trick's secret might be easy, you still need to practice it so that all of your movements look natural.

Here's what I mean: Think of something that you do really well right now. Something that you do so well that you don't even have to think about it!

Some of those things might include:

- Riding your bike
- Walking or running
- Playing your favorite video game

When I say that 'you don't have to think about doing these things, what I mean is that when you decide to do one of those things, you just start doing them once you make the decision.

For many people reading this book, walking is something you do without thinking about every little step. Let's say you are going to get up and walk to your kitchen to get a snack. You have to stand up, turn your body toward the kitchen, and start moving your muscles for one leg to take a step, then move the muscles of your other leg to take another step, and you keep doing it until you reach the kitchen.

Oh, and you have to maintain your balance for the whole trip!

I know what some of you reading this book are thinking: "Dude, you're weird! Of course I don't have to think about keeping my balance. I'm just walking!"

But that's the thing: You probably don't remember way back when you were just a little baby, when just standing up without falling over was a really big deal. And when you walked, you were all wobbly and stuff and grabbing chairs, a couch, curtains, or a grownup's legs all to stay upright while you walked.

It's no big deal to you now because you have practiced so much that it has become super easy for you.

That's what you want for your magic: for every move to look like it's something you have done a zillion times before. If you haven't practiced much, what happens is your movements become slow, you hesitate... and someone watching your tricks knows that you are doing something sneaky. They might not know exactly what you are doing but they will know you are doing something to make the magic happen.

So practice! Whatever moves your magic trick requires, do it so many times that you can do it without thinking about it... just like walking, riding your bike, or playing your favorite video game.

Rule #2 - Practice in front of a mirror!

When you start practicing, you'll need to practice in front of a mirror. This is so you can make sure that the way the magic trick looks when you are doing any sneaky stuff doesn't actually look like you are doing sneaky stuff.

Without using a mirror, you could be practicing your tricks in a way that really doesn't look magical at all. So a mirror will help you be able to make sure you are practicing the magic in the right way.

Here's another thing to think about: Have your mirror set up so you can see the moves in the same way that someone watching your magic will see those moves.

What I mean by that is this... if your mirror is very small and you have it leaning against your bedroom wall and you stand in front of it doing your magic, you are going to sort of be looking down at the reflection in the mirror. Most of the time, that is not going to be a good way to practice because most magic is not made for that kind of angle.

So when using your mirror, set it up so that when you look at the mirror's surface, it's the same view your friends will have as they watch you on Zoom.

Rule #3 - Practice in front of a camera!

Once you have practiced so much that you can do your tricks without thinking about them, and you have checked to make sure they look good in the mirror, then it's time to take the mirror away and keep practicing, but this time, practice in front of a camera.

Maybe you can set up your phone and record your magic that way. Or maybe your mom or dad or someone else you know has a video camera (or a phone) that they can use to record your magic.

You might be reading this thinking, "If I have practiced a bunch of times so my magic looks great in the mirror, why do I need to record it with a phone or camera?"

Here's the thing: By practicing your magic over and over in front of a mirror, you eventually get used to it so much that when you take the mirror away, it can really mess up your performing!

I'll tell you a story about how I almost really hurt myself when I was learning a magic trick by just using a mirror but without recording myself with my phone or camera.

I was practicing a new magic trick that involved me floating myself in the air! This was such a cool magic trick—it looked to the audience like I was floating about three feet in the air!

I had practiced this trick SO much for weeks in front of my mirror, and it looked really good, and I thought I was ready to do this trick in front of live audiences. So, I brought the trick with me to a show, and when it came time for me to do the trick and I started floating, I looked up and expected to see my reflection in a mirror.

Boy, was I in for a surprise! Without being able to see my own reflection, my balance was off, and I almost fell down!

Now, the tricks that you are going to learn in this book are very safe, so you won't get hurt, but if you skip the camera or phone, you might have problems doing the trick correctly once you take the mirror away.

There is something else that recording your magic practice with a phone or camera gives you: You might notice things in the recording that you did not realize you were doing before.

I was working on a trick once, and every time it was time for me to do a sneaky move, I blinked my eyes so I never actually watched myself doing the sneaky move. That means that I was really fooling myself because I was doing the move wrong, and for some reason, my brain was making me blink my eyes during that important move.

When I saw my recordings of me practicing that trick, I suddenly saw what was happening.

Learn how to do the trick, practice in front of a mirror until everything looks great, then take the mirror away and practice in front of a camera or phone.

Rule #4 - Misdirection

Misdirection means that you do something to get the people who are watching your magic to look somewhere else while you are doing the secret moves.

Here's something super important: When you do misdirection, it means that you get the audience watching your magic to look somewhere else... but the people watching you should not know that you are trying to get them to look away.

Confused? If so, that's okay, because I know I was when I first started learning magic!

Here's two ways of trying to misdirect someone watching your magic and you can guess which one you think is better.

Magic Trick #1: There is a magician onstage, and he's holding a metal spoon in his hand. The trick he wants to show his audience is a metal spoon that will bend by magic. He tells the audience he is going to cause the spoon to bend with the power of his mind. He tells the audience to keep watching the spoon, no matter what happens. A second later, there is a very loud explosion on the other side of the stage. When the noise dies down, the magician once again holds up the spoon—it is bent completely in half!

Magic Trick #2: A magician is showing some people a card trick. He asks one person (let's pretend the person who is picking a card is named Nancy) to pick a card out of the deck, write their name on the card, and then put the card back in the middle of the deck. The deck of cards is sitting on a table between the magician and the people watching the trick. He looks at Nancy and says, "Nancy, would you be amazed if I could find your card?" When Nancy hears her name, she looks at the magician's face and says yes. After hearing Nancy answer, the magician waves his hand in a magical way, and asks Nancy to pick up the top card of the deck. Amazingly, it's Nancy's signed card!

Which magician do you think did a better job at misdirection? Think about it for a moment...

If you said Magician #2, you are right!

Both of those stories were from real magic shows with real magicians.

With Magician #1, he was just trying to be funny and do something silly. When the explosion happened, the audience looked toward the explosion, and when they all looked away, that's when the magician bent the spoon.

When the audience watching turned away from the loud noise and back to the magician, they saw the spoon had become bent while they were looking away, and at that moment, everyone laughed because they knew the magician bent the spoon while they were distracted by the loud noise.

No one was fooled by it, and the magician was not trying to fool anyone. He just thought it would be funny.

With Magician #2, the trick was to do a secret move to get Nancy's card from the middle of the deck (where she put it) onto the top of the deck without the audience realizing it. He had to distract Nancy and get her to look away from the deck of cards long enough to do his secret move without Nancy realizing he did anything.

How did he do it?

By using her name.

There is something magical about our names! When we hear our name spoken out loud, we almost always pay attention.

Think about this: Have you ever been in school or in a store and you hear someone calling your name and you turn to look and you realize it was someone calling out to another kid who had the same name as you? Hearing our name just gets our attention.

That's just one way of misdirection. There are many others! For instance, magic wands. If a professional magician uses a magic wand, he or she is using it for one of two reasons:

1. To be funny
2. To misdirect your attention

When I perform magic at my school assemblies, I might use funny magic wands that change color or fall apart just to cause everyone to laugh. But many magicians might use a magic wand to distract someone so they can do a secret move.

The magician might have some cups upside down on a table, and under each cup is one red ball. The magician might then say, "I need to get something really important—my magic wand." As he or she reaches over to get the magic wand with one hand, the other hand is doing a secret move to make one of the red balls disappear from under one cup and reappear under a different cup.

Here's the thing about doing magic over the internet: It's a lot harder to misdirect someone's attention while they are watching you on a computer screen. Fortunately, the tricks in this book are great for the internet and really don't need much misdirection.

But learning about misdirection is important to get really good at magic, especially if you ever decide to do magic for people who are watching you live, not over the internet.

Rule #5 - Never repeat a trick

This is one of the most important rules in magic! Well... uh... they are all important! But this is the most important rule we are going to talk about right now. Yeah, that makes sense!

So much of what makes magic fun is surprise! And when someone sees a good magic trick the first time, being surprised is one of the things that makes magic work so well.

When a person sees the same trick twice, they know what is going to happen, so they start looking around, trying to figure out how the trick works. People aren't always trying to spoil the fun or be mean... people are just curious. They want to know stuff.

There is something about people wanting to understand stuff. With kids, it happens even more. You probably don't remember this, but almost every kid on the planet is super-duper curious when they are really young.

A kid might ask her mom, "Why is the sky blue?"

The mom might say, "Because of the atmosphere."

The kid might then ask, "Why do dogs have fur?"

The mom might answer, "To help keep him warm."

Then the kid might ask, "Why is there water in the world?"

The mom might say, "Because water supports life."

The kid might say, "Well, for one thing, people need to drink water to stay alive."

And the conversation might go on for another thirty questions. People of any age are curious, but the younger the person, the more curious they often are. There's just something about people's brains that makes them curious and want to understand what they see or experience.

By repeating a magic trick, people watching will no longer be surprised and will usually try to figure out how the trick works.

Rule #6 - Think about angles

Angles? Like geometry? Like math? Sort of!

In this case, when a magician is showing a magic trick, there will usually be a position to watch the trick that is best for the magician, which means that people watching from a certain position won't see anything that needs to be hidden.

There will also be other positions where if a person watched, they might see something that would reveal the secret to them.

If you imagine the magician is at the center of a clock, and the audience can watch the trick from, or even between, any number on the clock, it makes sense why magicians call this "watching your angles" because for most tricks, there will be positions on that clock where watching the trick will keep the secret to the trick a secret, but other positions would let someone watching see the secret.

So if you think about it like that, it is a little like geometry!

Now, there are some tricks that don't have any bad positions where the people watching the magic can see the secrets. Magicians talk about those tricks being "angle-proof," or "being able to do the trick surrounded."

Most of the tricks in this book have "very good angles," which means it is easier to hide the secret, especially on the internet.

Really, though, it is a lot easier to do magic on the internet because the people watching you only have one place to watch the magic: right in front! When I am doing magic for live shows, I have to make sure people don't try to sneak behind me and see things they shouldn't.

With every trick in this book, I will explain what angles you need to be careful of, and on the videos, I will also show you what to pay attention to with your angles.

Rule #7 - Think about how to string tricks together

Every person reading this book is interested in magic for different reasons. Every reason is a good reason to get into magic. Here are a few reasons why you might be reading this book:

☺ Maybe you want to learn secrets of magic because you want to know how they work.

☺   Maybe you want to show your family or friends a couple of tricks and hear them say, "Wow! That was really neat!"

☺   Or maybe you want to learn enough about magic to perform a complete show!

All of those reasons (and many I did not list!) are all great reasons to be reading this book. If you are someone who wants to learn enough about magic to perform a complete show, then you will want to think about how to put several tricks together into a show.

There are a lot of things to talk about when it comes to putting an entire show together, and I could write entire books just about that, but for right now, I'll just give some basic ideas to putting an entire show together.

Remember this, though: There are a lot of ways to put an entire show together. In this section, I'm giving just one way, the way that works for me.

Most magicians' shows start with a really fast, surprising, visual trick. That's great because it grabs everyone's attention and convinces everyone to pay attention to the show.

Starting off the show that takes a long time to get to the magic is not a good idea because the people watching want to see magic right away. So your first trick should be something quick and one that does not need a lot of counting or explaining. The Two Quarters, One Dime trick in the Money Tricks chapter of this book is a great example of a good opening trick because the magic happens in just a few seconds!

The middle of the show (in other words, the tricks that happen after the opening trick but before your last trick) is where you want to have your longer tricks... that is, tricks where you have to count objects, or ask the people watching your magic to select things, or just tricks that take longer to do.

The last trick should be your best trick, the one trick that you do better than any other trick, and hopefully your most amazing trick, too. Also, if at all possible, your last trick should be one that does not involve volunteers so that when the trick is over, you are alone onstage, ready to take your bow and close the show.

This simple show structure is an easy way to get started organizing your tricks, and after you get more experience, you'll eventually develop a 'feel' for how to organize your show.

Rule #8 - Make moves look like real life

When I am talking about making moves look like real life, you might be thinking, "You are one strange dude! You can't make magic look like real life because there is no magic in real life, it's a trick!"

Yup you are right, but hear me out... in magic, there are certain moves that we have to do, and if we do our best to make them look natural, that is going to go a long way toward convincing someone that magic is happening.

Here's an example: Later on in this book, you are going to learn some sleight of hand magic, that is—magic where using your hand's movements in a certain way is what makes the magic happen instead of a trick prop or hidden string or whatever.

One of the tricks involves simply showing your audience a coin in one hand and then reaching over and taking the coin by closing your other hand's fingers around it. When you open that hand, the coin has disappeared!

What's really going on is that the coin stays behind in the first hand... it never actually goes into your second hand.

The thing that makes that trick so magical is how natural the moves are. I don't know who invented this trick (it's called the French Drop... maybe it was invented by a French dude?), but whoever he was, he really studied something simple—taking an object from one hand into the other, and doing the very best he could to make it look like he was really taking the coin in his other hand.

The more natural he did this, the more magical the trick looked.

How do you do this? Simple: In the case of making a coin disappear from your hand, it's a really good idea to practice REALLY taking the coin in your other hand. Watch your self in a mirror doing this. Watch yourself on video really taking that coin. Then, when you do the magic moves, do your very best to make your movements look just like you did when you actually took the coin in your other hand.

This idea of making your magic movements look like real life is one of the most important things you can do to make your magic look great!

Rule #9 - What to do if people want to look at props

When people want to look at magic props while you are performing, it often means they are suspicious, so if you get asked that a lot, it is a really good idea to record yourself doing the tricks and see if you can make things look more natural in your movements.

Other things you can do include:

- Only do magic tricks over the internet. Since this magic book is titled Virtual Magic, you could do magic using Zoom or whatever, and people would never get a chance to look at your props!
- You could only do magic that uses regular things you can gather from around your house. After you

do something magical, your audience can look at everything, and there is nothing sneaky to be seen!

- Go right into another magic trick before your audience has a chance to even think about asking you if they can look at your props.
- While everyone is saying "Wow!" or "That was really cool!" you put the props away.
- Simply tell them, "Magic is all about that awesome feeling of amazement, so that's way more important than props."

Rule #10 - How to handle if people ask how a trick is done or shout out how it's done

When some people ask how a trick is done, they just might be curious. I have had grownups ask me, "Wow! How did you do that?" after I show them magic, and most of the time, the person asking is not really asking me to tell them how the trick is done. They are really saying, "That was amazing!"

It's sort of like when a group of people is watching a football game together. If there is a really exciting play, one person might say to someone right next to them, "Wow! Did you see that?"

In that case, of course both people saw the exciting play. When the first person asked the question, he really was not trying to find out if the other person saw the play... he was really just talking about how amazed they were at the exciting play.

So the first thing you might say after someone asks you how a magic trick works is just to say, "I know, that's really amazing, right? I felt the same way you do when I saw this the first time!"

That will work a lot of the time. But if someone keeps asking, saying things like, "No, really! I want to know! You've got to tell me!" then there are a lot of things you can say.

Here's a few ideas:

- ☺ "I worked on this trick really hard and I don't want to spoil it for you."
- ☺ "Once you learn the secret, it's not as amazing."
- ☺ "I made a promise when I learned magic never to tell the secret. You don't want me to break my promise, do you?"
- ☺ "Can you keep a secret? So can I."

What about when someone just shouts out the secret to the trick?

Usually when someone does that, they are just taking a guess and saying out loud what their guess is. It does not always mean that they are right.

It reminds me of a really cool rope trick I learned. It's really fun, amazing, and surprising. And not a lot of people have seen it. By that I mean that it's a pretty hard trick so not a lot of magicians want to perform it.

But there are a LOT of amazing rope tricks... like thousands of rope tricks! I'm not making that up. And many of those rope tricks start the same way: The magician has to take out a big piece of rope.

Because a lot of people have seen magicians do rope tricks, as soon as I take out a piece of rope, I almost always hear someone say, "I know that trick." That's usually just their way of saying, "Oh, I think I might have seen this before."

For my rope trick, I usually just smile and keep going.

So if someone says they know how your trick is done, you can just keep going without saying anything to that person. They might just be really good at figuring out magic tricks. Or they could be wrong and just saying what they think is the right answer,

If someone says out loud how they think the trick is done (it doesn't matter if they are right or wrong) here are a few things you can say:

☺ "That solution is a pretty good one. There are hundreds of ways to do every magic trick. I can't tell you which way this trick works today. It's a secret."

☺ "That's pretty good. Can we keep the secrets to these tricks between us so everyone else enjoys the show?"

☺ "Wow, that's a pretty good guess. After the show, you and I can talk about it privately."

But if someone says, "Hey, I know how that trick is done! I saw something sticking out of your hand," then it might mean you need to practice more.

If that happens, it's okay. People are not perfect. Ever since I started performing magic professionally, I have performed over 6000 shows (that's a lot!) and to this day, I still make mistakes.

It might not feel good when you are trying to show someone magic and you mess up, but you can learn from it and get better. Even the best in the world at something (whether it's magic, football, painting, singing, whatever) make mistakes. When they make a mistake, they figure out what they did wrong, and then they fix it.

So that's ten things you can do to make your magic more than just about the secrets. Master these ten rules, and you will be well on your way to becoming a really good magician.

But what if there was a way to become a GREAT magician? That's what the next chapter is all about!

Chapter 3:

The Top 10 Secrets of Great Magic

Magic is so much more than just the secrets. When a magician only thinks about the secrets, that means the only thing the trick can do is fool someone. Here's the deal: People do not like to be fooled but they DO like to be entertained!

Think about it like this... when you go to the movies and watch the Avengers or Harry Potter do something amazing during that movie, you know that it's all special effects. You might not know exactly what kind of special effect, but you know that what is happening onscreen is make-believe.

Magic is the same way. Most people watching magic know that it is not real, but they watch the tricks for the same reason they watch a movie: to have a good time and see something that looks impossible.

If you just want to learn the secrets, that's perfectly fine. That's how I got into magic—I wanted to learn the secrets.

But if you want to really amaze your friends and family and hear them say, "Wow! That was amazing! How did you do that?" then you'll really like this chapter. There are really important things that are more than just secrets that are the way to get those kinds of reactions.

If you use the things in this chapter, people will enjoy watching your magic a lot more. In fact, I'm going to reveal ten awesome secrets to great magic! Here we go…

Secret #1 - Look into their eyes

When you look into someone's eyes, you are showing confidence. That's one of the things that people like most about good magic… confidence!

People watching magic like knowing that the person doing the magic is really good at what they are doing… otherwise they may not want to watch.

Here's a story to kind of show you what I mean. Back in 2001, the owner of WWE pro wrestling, Vince McMahon, wanted to start his own American football league, like the NFL.

The problem was—the NFL had all of the best players. So the XFL put it's teams together with players that were not quite good enough for the NFL. Maybe they were a little slower, a little older, or maybe they couldn't throw as far as NFL players.

When the XFL started playing, people didn't really like watching the games because the XFL had some really goofy rules, which made it harder for the players to play well.

Pretty soon, not very many people were watching the XFL. The players started losing their confidence because not many people wanted to watch, so they didn't play as well as they could.

So it's the same thing with magic. People don't need to believe you are one of the best magicians in the world in order to watch you and enjoy what you do... but they do need to believe you are really good at what you do and are confident in your abilities.

The other reason why it is good to look your audience in their eyes while you are performing is so you can watch THEIR eyes! I have a certain card trick that I do, and it has a special move I need to do twice for the trick. Right before I do the move, I always watch everyone's eyes to make sure they are not looking at my hands when I do the move.

Here's one more reason to look in their eyes when you are performing: The more you look into people's eyes, the more confident you will really become!

Confidence comes with practice. Confidence comes from doing something correctly so many times that you have that special feeling of "Yeah, I got this!" filling up your entire body. And confidence is something that is important in every part of your life.

Let's face it: Because you are reading this book, it means I'm not in the same room with you, so I can't talk to you or ask you questions and hear your answers... so I don't know what you want to be when you grow up.

Maybe you want to be a doctor, or a veterinarian, or a singer, or a teacher, or a magician. But I DO know one thing: Being confident is important no matter what you want to be when you grow up.

The best part? Learning to be confident by doing magic tricks is FUN!

Secret #2 - Hold your head up high!

This is right there with Secret #1!

Did you ever hear your teacher or your mom or dad tell you to stop slouching or to stand up straight?

Okay, this might seem like a weird thing to write about in a magic book because your parents or teacher might be telling you those things to help you with your posture, and that doesn't have anything to do with magic... does it?

Actually, it does! If you are performing magic with your head down and you are kind of slouching, you won't look very confident in your magic, and like I wrote about before, confidence is super-important for everything in life!

Here's the other thing: If you are holding your head high, that will help you direct people to look and react the way you want them to. I am not talking about giving someone who is watching your magic orders to go stand someplace else or anything like that... but when you hold your head high, that does kind of happen without you really trying!

This is kind of hard to explain in a book like this, but the WAY you talk to someone is in some ways more important than the actual words you use.

Check out some magicians on YouTube. Find and watch a magician who is bent over his table doing card tricks. The ones who are always slouched over looking at their hands don't look very confident. Then find some magicians doing card tricks who hold up their heads straight as they do their magic. They are looking at the people watching them way more than they are watching their own hands. They look more confident!

When someone holds their head up high (and look into other peoples' eyes), they develop what's called a "magnetic personality."

No, I'm not talking about turning yourself into a great big magnet and causing metal objects to stick to you! Having a "magnetic personality" means that you are so confident that people just realize it and want to pay attention to you. And people who have that kind of a personality do it without coming off as stuck-up... they do it just by feeling really good about themselves and helping other people feel good about themselves too!

Here's the BEST part: You can have a magnetic personality by being confident... and it doesn't matter if you are short or tall, girl or boy, Black or White or Asian or Hispanic or something else... it's all in how you feel about yourself.

I remember once seeing a magician on *Penn & Teller: Fool Us.* He was a magician who was born without hands. Most magicians would think you couldn't do sleight of hand magic without hands. But this guy worked and worked and worked on special moves he created all by himself that he could do with just his arms, no hands. He developed the confidence in himself to do something that no one thought he could do, and he did a great job on the show and not only amazed the audience, but also fooled Penn & Teller as well!

And if you watch this magician, his name is Mahdi Gilbert, you'll see that he holds his head high!

There are a lot more things in this chapter that you can do in order to create a magnetic personality, and they are all things that YOU can do for yourself... and the best part is— no one can take those things away from you. Ever!

Secret #3 - Speak clearly

If people can't hear you, they won't be able to follow the plot of your magic.

For me, this was very hard growing up. I had a pretty bad stutter, and even to this day as a grownup, there are a few letter combinations that are a little hard for me to say.

This is another secret that helps build your confidence, Mumbling or not speaking clearly can make people think you are not confident, even if you are actually confident.

So, if you are like I was and are very shy, or if you just have a habit of mumbling, how can you get better?

Like everything else, it comes down to practice. Start by listening to how confident people speak. You can listen to magicians, or actors, or your teachers. Basically, you can listen to any person who talks to other people as part of their job as a performer or teacher.

Listen to how they say certain words. Notice how their mouth moves as they say certain words. Then you can say some of the same words, record yourself, and listen to it.

Practice speaking over and over, and work on it as often as you can.

Here's the deal: Being a clear speaker is another one of those things that can help you in life no matter what job you decide to do. Maybe you'll become a magician like me. Maybe you'll become a teacher. Speaking clearly is important no matter what you do.

And another thing... if you speak clearly and people can understand you, they will respect you more.

No one was ever born a good performer. No one was ever born a good speaker.

It all comes down to practice.

Secret #4 - Listen to what people say

Here's a 'not-so-secret' secret: People are most interested in themselves!

I know, big surprise, right?

So if you want people to be interested in you, what you are doing, and your magic, it will help a lot if you listen to other people.

This is kind of advanced-level magic stuff, but there are too many magicians who are not very nice to people who help them out with a trick. The magician may tell them where to stand, what to do, where to put something, all kinds of things.

But even though some of these magicians work with a lot of people and have a lot of volunteers during their shows, they don't really act like they care very much about the people helping them. They just want people to hold a rope, or pick a card, or say a number, or something like that.

I don't know if this is the very first magic book you have ever read or if you have read a lot of other magic books, but even if you are a beginner, you can be a better magician than these magicians I'm talking about. And it's really simple! Ready?

All you have to do is listen when people talk.

That's it!

So when you ask someone to help you with a magic trick, take an extra moment or two and talk to them. What kinds of things can you talk to them about?

Watch other famous magicians as they talk to their volunteers. If the magician is world-famous, he or she might ask the person what their name is and where they are from.

Since we are talking about doing magic virtually in this book, you may wind up doing magic for people you don't know who live in other parts of your country or even in other countries around the world. In those cases, if you don't already know those people, then it's a really good idea to ask them their name and where they are from.

Of course, if you are just starting off in magic, you will probably start off by performing tricks for your friends and family.

In that case, it might seem kind of silly to ask them what their name is or where they are from. But you can still ask them questions. What kind of things can you ask them?

Here's just a few ideas:

- ☺ You can ask them if they like magic.
- ☺ Ask them if they've ever seen magic before.

☺ Ask them if they have ever seen magic over the internet before.

☺ Ask them if they have a favorite magic trick that they've seen.

Also, if you are performing magic for your family and friends, since they know you, they might ask YOU questions, and you can listen to what they ask and then respond.

The whole point is to talk to the people helping you with your magic... and listen to what they say.

Here's the thing: I'll bet you have been talking to someone before, maybe a friend, a teacher, maybe even your mom or dad, and the person you are talking to is doing ALL of the talking, and you are just wishing they would pause and stop talking for a second because you have something you really want to say or ask, and then the person who is talking FINALLY stops talking, and you get to say or ask whatever it is you wanted, and what happened?

The person says, "Yeah," or something else really short, and then they start talking again.

If that ever happened to you, how did it make you feel? It happened to me a lot as a kid, and it still happens to me as a grownup. It doesn't feel good.

I don't think people really want to make us feel bad. I just think sometimes, we get so excited about what we want to say that we forget that talking with people in the best way means we are each talking AND listening.

So when you are performing your magic, and someone says something to you, look them in their eyes and pay attention to what they are saying. And after they finish talking, count to "one" inside your brain before you start talking again. Just that little pause, plus looking them in their eye, will help you get used to really listening to what people are saying.

Now, of course, if someone is shouting out how the trick is done or something like that, then you can just ignore what they say, but this secret, the secret of listening, is important for most of the time when talking to people, not just when performing magic.

Not only is listening to what people say the right thing to do, but it can also give you ideas for some really good things to say for your magic. Here's what I mean.

Recently, I was teaching one of my Discover Magic online classes, and one of my students was graduating (in Discover Magic, there are four courses: a Green Wand course, a Purple Wand course, an Orange Wand course, and a Blue Wand course) ,and on graduation day, all students get to perform any magic trick they want.

The trick that this particular student performed was one that I had taught her, but she had written a completely new story, or script, to go along with it. And her story was better than my story. She was 8 years old and just starting in magic. I have been performing magic for years and years... but her story was better than mine.

I was so proud of her! I told her over and over again how impressed I was with her story.

The thing is, if I had not been listening closely, I might not have realized just how great her story was.

Like anything else, good listening takes practice, and it is something that can help you everywhere in life.

Maybe your mom or dad asked you to do some chores around the house. Maybe your teacher in school is giving you a very special homework assignment, one that has a lot of important details that you need to pay attention to. Maybe, when you are a grownup, someone you work with (like your boss) gives you some very important instructions.

So, practice listening carefully.

Secret #4 - Perform what interests your audience

What kind of magic do you like?

Do you like tricks with coins, cards, or string? Or maybe you like tricks with numbers, puzzles, or pictures?

If someone were to ask me what kind of magic I like best, I would tell them that I like stage magic the best. Stage magic is kind of between great big illusions and close-up magic.

For the actual tricks, I like tricks that are surprising, funny, and make it look like my volunteers are the ones doing the magic.

When you are just starting off in magic and you are showing magic to your family and friends, it's okay to show them the kind of tricks that you like. After you have been doing magic for a while, you will notice that certain people you perform for like certain kinds of tricks but they don't like others.

Here's what I mean: When I was first learning magic, I liked magic tricks that were kind of spooky or creepy. One trick that I had was a little doll made of straw. I would tell a story about the doll, and how an old witch used the doll to do some bad things. Then I would place the little doll in my hand... and after a few moments, it would stand up all by itself!

It was a really cool trick, but after performing it a bunch of times, I noticed that my mom didn't like that trick because she didn't like things that were creepy or scary.

After you have been performing magic for a while, if you have been listening to the people you are performing for, you may notice how they react or what they say when you do certain kinds of magic.

Maybe your friends get really excited when you take out a deck of cards and start doing magic. Maybe they don't get excited when you take out a piece of string. Pay attention to what people say and how they react, and when it's time to pick new magic tricks, try to remember how the people you perform most for react.

Me? I perform mostly on stage on front of 400-500 kids at a time. There have been times when I try to show them a magic trick that is really small, and because it is so little, not everyone can really see it to enjoy it.

Want to know how I know?

I listen.

Yup, that secret again!

I hear the kids start talking to themselves, saying things like, "I can't see that," or "What is it? I couldn't tell what was happening." Or they don't even talk about the trick and just start talking to each other because they are bored.

So for big audiences, I learned pretty fast that there are certain tricks I can't do because not everyone can see them.

On the other hand, I have bigger tricks that everyone can see. I have one trick with a sketchpad. I draw a face on the sketchpad, and the eyes and mouth start moving! Then I can tear off the paper from the pad, give it to one of the teachers, and all the kids can see it hanging on the wall by the main office after the show.

For that trick, I tried performing it a few times, and I listened to how everyone reacted: Everyone loved it, so I kept performing it.

So you can do the same thing: Listen to your audiences. If your mom doesn't like a certain trick but your friends do, then do that trick for your friends. If your friends don't like a certain trick you do but your dad does, then just show that trick to your dad... and when it comes time to show your dad another trick, try to find tricks just like that the last one that he liked to show him.

Of course, there will be certain tricks that you perform that EVERYONE likes! Those tricks are the best, and I always try to find more like that.

Then there may be tricks you try that no one likes. I remember growing up when I wanted to learn magic that there was this one trick that it seemed like everyone I met was doing. It was a card trick, and it felt really boring to me. It involved a lot of counting cards from one pile to another and back again.

It didn't feel magical. It just felt like a lot of counting, and every time I saw someone do that trick, I felt my mind wandering. So I never perform that trick when I do magic.

By paying attention to what kind of tricks your audience likes and doing those kinds of tricks for them, they will enjoy your magic a lot more and will look forward to seeing more of your magic.

Secret #5 - If they don't like a trick; change, try to make it better, or let it go

I have to admit, for me this was one of the hardest lessons I had to learn.

If your audiences don't like a trick, there are a lot of things you can do. There have been many magic tricks that I invested a lot into, whether it was spending a lot of money for the trick, or the trick being very hard to learn, and after I perform the trick several times, the audience just doesn't like it.

Here's the deal: If you are just starting out in magic, there is an excellent chance you will show your friends and family a lot of different tricks. Friends and family members are almost always the audience that a brand-new magician has when starting out, especially if you are young and still in school. And that's great! That's how I got started.

What this means is simple: You might not have the ability to do a trick 10 times or more to see if it's a really good trick for you. One of the basic rules in magic is to not repeat a trick for the same audience, so that means if your only audience is your family, you really can't show them the same trick a bunch of times to find out if it's a really good trick.

So what can you do?

You can take notes on how everyone reacted when you showed them a certain trick. Compare the reaction of your latest trick to reactions for other tricks you've done. Listen to what questions people ask you afterward.

Eventually, if you stick with magic, you'll find you have more and more people you can show your tricks to. As that happens, show these new audiences the same tricks. You'll get better and better at each trick, and the more times you do a trick for an audience, the more you can keep track of which tricks get the best reactions.

When you find yourself doing the same tricks all the time for different audiences, that's when you can really begin to notice which tricks get the best reactions.

If you find that every single time you do a certain trick it gets a really good reaction, then it's definitely a trick you want to keep. I have some tricks I have been doing for 30 years!

Then, with other tricks, you'll find that no matter what you do, people just don't enjoy them, and that's okay too.

If there's a trick you like but it doesn't get a good reaction, maybe you can change how you do the trick. Maybe you need to record yourself doing the trick so you can find out if you are doing anything wrong. Maybe You can change the story you tell.

Once, I had a really expensive trick that just was not getting a good reaction. I was doing the trick without talking and just playing some music while I did the trick. I tried playing a different song for the trick, and suddenly everyone reacted better to the trick. That was 12 yeas ago and I still do the trick to this day, and in fact, it's the final closing trick for one of my shows!

I'm talking about all of these things because giving up on a trick after you perform it one time really isn't the way to becoming a great magician. A great magician will try something, and if doesn't work, try something else, and keep going until there is nothing left to try.

It's easy to give up. It's harder, but much more rewarding, to keep trying.

Does this mean that by trying harder, you will always succeed? No, it doesn't, but giving up too soon means you'll never succeed.

There are some tricks that I have given up on, or as I prefer to say; tricks I have let go.

Sometimes, a trick may not fit your personality. Recently, I was teaching one of my Discover Magic online classes and one of my students and I were talking about finding magic that fits you as a person.

You may not know this yet, but I'm a pretty goody guy when I perform. I like making people laugh and feel good about themselves. There are other magicians, famous magicians, who are very serious, and sometimes even a little scary.

I asked my student, who has seen me perform and teach a LOT of magic, if she thought it would be a good idea for me to try being scary when I perform magic.

She thought about it for a moment and finally said, "No, I don't think so." You know what? She's absolutely right! If I tried to be scary when I did my magic, it just wouldn't fit me.

My whole point of bringing all of this up is there are so many things to try and think about before you decide to stop performing a magic trick.

Before you give up on a trick, here are some things to try:

- ☺ Record yourself doing the trick so you can make sure you are doing the moves perfectly.
- ☺ Change the script (the words you say while performing the trick) to see if a different story would help.
- ☺ Even if you are doing the moves correctly, make sure your angles are good for the trick... in other words, make sure that when you perform the trick, no one can see anything they are not supposed to.
- ☺ Think about whether the trick is the kind of magic your audience likes. Your mom may not like it if you do a scary magic trick. Your 4-year old sister probably does not understand magic.

After you have tried these things, if the trick still is not getting the reactions it should, then it may be okay to let that trick go and work on a different one. The point is, don't give up too soon.

Secret #6 - Smile

This may not seem like a really big secret to becoming a master magician, but this is huge! And the really cool thing is this: Like pretty much everything in this book, this will help you in so many places, not just magic!

Here's why smiling when you do magic is so important: When you smile, people watching you feel better about themselves. It's a really cool 'science-y' thing that goes on inside people. When they see someone smile, it makes them want to smile. It just helps peoples' moods.

And the really wild thing is this: When you smile, it helps YOUR mood too! I don't mean for this to turn into a science book (although I do have science books too!), but when you smile, it does something really cool in your brain that helps you feel better.

So, if you ever feel kind of sad, there are a lot of things you can do (like talking to a trusted grownup), and one of the easiest things to do is just smile.

When you smile while doing magic, it will make people feel better while watching your magic. It's amazing!

Secret #7 - Asking if they want to see magic

This secret is all about being polite. Here's what I mean...

Years ago, before I started performing magic in schools, I used to perform magic at corporate events. "Corporate Events" are when all of the grownups who work together at a company get together after work for a holiday party or an important meeting to talk about business stuff for the company.

I used to get hired by these companies to do magic when these people were standing around drinking their Pepsi drinks waiting for dinner to come. I'd be told to go to each table and show the people at each table 3 or 4 quick magic tricks as part of the entertainment for that night.

Most of the time, the people enjoyed my little show for their table. But a few times, I'd walk up to a table and the people sitting there were having a very serious conversation, and maybe one of the people would look really sad.

I'd ask the table of people if they wanted to see some magic. Sometimes, even though they looked sad, they would say yes, and I would do my magic, and they would smile. I felt good because I was able to help some of these people get their minds off of their troubles for a little while.

At some tables, however, some of the people might say, "No, we really don't want to see any magic right now."

Maybe they wanted to continue talking. Maybe they didn't really like magic. Maybe they had seen other magicians who had been rude or mean (I'll talk more about that a little later).

So when someone said that to me, what do you think I did?

If you guessed that I thanked them and politely walked away, you're absolutely right!

If someone does not want to see my magic, it doesn't mean they don't like ME, it just might mean they don't like magic, or they are not in the mood for magic, or whatever.

A great magician respects his audiences enough to not show them magic if they don't want to see it.

I'm pretty old, so I have read a lot of magic books. Most of them just teach secrets, but some of them try to teach other really important stuff, like I'm trying to do with this book. Some of those books would give advice to the magicians reading the book on ways to get people to watch your magic when you walk up to their table.

Some of the books would say to pretend you are a waiter for the restaurant. People will always pay attention to a waiter because they want their food. The books would say to start talking about the food and suddenly do a magic trick.

Another book would say to walk up to the table holding a twenty-dollar bill and ask if anyone dropped it. And before anyone answered, suddenly you were supposed to do something magical with the bill, so people were suddenly watching your magic without being asked to.

I never liked any of those ideas. I always though the best thing to do was simply ask if they wanted to see magic.

It kind of reminds me of a time a few years ago when my wife and I took a trip. We live in the state of New York. We were flying to Alaska to visit some friends. We had known these friends for a few years. On this trip, we were staying at their house, which is something we had never done before.

Well, the trip was not very fun. The friends told us everything we were going to do. They would ask us if we liked certain foods or certain TV shows, and even if we said no, they didn't care and would make us eat those foods and watch those TV shows. It was very uncomfortable because we did not have anywhere else to go until it was time for our airplane to take us back home several days later.

My wife and I were very confused by all of this because when friends come to visit us at our house, we always ask them what food they would like or what TV shows they want to watch. We will pick things that everyone (our friends and my wife and I) all like, so everyone is happy and comfortable.

It's the same thing with magic. By asking someone if they want to see your magic, you are showing yourself to be a great magician of character.

And if the person you ask says "No," remember, it doesn't mean they don't like you. It just means they don't want to see magic at that time. It reminds me of a really special phrase...

Secret #8 - Respect your audience

In many ways, this is the most important secret in this entire book. Respecting your audiences is the same as respecting people in life. Here's what I mean by that.

There are many ways to present magic. When I was growing up, most of the magicians I saw wore tuxedoes, just like what a man would wear when he was getting married. Most of those magicians smiled a lot and were very polite to their audiences.

As I got older, I became aware of other ways of presenting magic. A magician named David Blaine became very popular by doing magic on the street. In other words, he was dressed in casual clothes, usually jeans and a black t-shirt, and he would walk up to a person standing outside and show them some magic.

Blaine became very popular, and even though he was a different kind of magician, he was still polite to his audiences, even if he acted a little creepy at times. But his style of magic led to some things that were not good for the art.

More and more magicians loved the idea of "street magic," of going up to random people in public and doing magic for them. But a lot of these new magicians wanted to shock people or scare people.

And as David Blaine became more and more popular, he also began doing scary or gross kind of magic tricks that would make the people he was performing for very uncomfortable.

I remember when, 20 years ago, a trick came out called The Web. It was a trick where you asked someone to hold out their hands and you, as the magician, would out blank cards into the person's hand. Then, after talking about spiders, those blank cards suddenly had pictures of spider webs on them. It was very magical.

But then, the end of the trick was designed to make people scream: After seeing the spider webs magically appear on the cards, the person was told to turn their hands over and they would see a big hairy spider on the back of their hands.

The spider was just plastic, but it still scared people. And many people have a really bad fear of spiders.

That trick was an example of what is sometimes called "shock magic," and many people find it to be scary or uncomfortable.

To me, all of this is really bad for magic. I feel magic should be done to make people feel good.

So when you are thinking of magic to learn, think about doing tricks that you can perform in a way that is respectful for audiences. In other words, treat others how you want to be treated.

If you are young and reading this and thinking, "Well, I like the idea of creepy magic and I think my friends would too." You might be right, and then it would be appropriate to show magic tricks to your friends like that, and they may enjoy them.

My point is—it's always best to treat your audience respectfully and in a way they enjoy. Even if you would do a scary trick like The Web for your friends, you could be respectful by saying before you do the trick, "Who here wants to see a really scary magic trick?" And then when you get a volunteer, you would tell the person, "Okay, this is going to be really scary! Are you sure you want to do it?"

So at least that way, you are doing your best to be respectful. That way, your volunteer knows something scary might happen and they are ready for it. In that case, it's sort of like going on a roller coaster: People who go on roller coasters know before they get on that it's supposed to be scary and fun, and if that is their idea of a good time, then they can enjoy it.

Another thing that some magicians do that is not very respectful is something called 'sucker tricks.' With these kinds of tricks, a magician will pretend to do one thing, usually that he or she will teach some magic, and then at the end of the trick, the magician reveals a completely different kind of trick and that the magician was never really going to teach any magic.

The whole point of a sucker trick is for the magician to be able to say to the audience, "Ha! I fooled you." Even if the magician does not say those exact words, the audience still gets the idea that the magician just wanted to fool them and then remind them that they were fooled.

To me, those kinds of tricks don't make the audience feel good about themselves.

Remember, when picking tricks to show people, always think to yourself, "How will the audience feel at the end of this trick?" Will they feel amazed? Will they laugh? Will they feel 'tricked?'

In my opinion, no one likes to be 'tricked' or 'fooled,' but people DO enjoy being 'amazed' or 'entertained.'

Think of how others feel first, and you'll be a great magician!

Secret #9 - Think of a good presentation

A 'presentation' in magic means how you are going to show your audience the trick.

The great thing about magic is that there are no limits to the kinds of ways you can show your magic.

For instance, you can tell a story with your magic. When I teach kids magic in my Discover Magic online classes, I will use stories a lot. For instance, in this book, one of the tricks I teach is how to float a dollar bill! This looks really amazing!

To set up the trick, I tell the audience that a few days ago, I met an alien! And I shook hands with this alien... now, everything I touch floats in the air, all because I shook hands with this alien!

Now, do my audiences really believe that I met an alien?

No, I don't think so.

But telling that little story made the magic more interesting to everyone. This is another one of those science-y things that I am not going to write much about, but there is something about peoples' brains that just enjoy a good story.

A long time ago, before people had created written language, they passed on all their information by talking and telling stories. So peoples' brains are still made to perk up and pay attention when someone starts telling a story.

Is storytelling the only way to present magic? Not at all.

Another way I will present magic is with music. Sometimes, when performing a trick, I won't say anything at all and just do the trick with music. In fact, one of my all-time favorite magic tricks is called the Dancing Hanky—in which a little hanky comes to life and dances about, on the floor, behind me, in a bottle, everywhere—and I do that trick with music.

You can even use music to do closeup card tricks! In fact, on the TV show *Penn & Teller: Fool Us*, a magician named Shin Lim fooled Penn & Teller twice by doing card magic set to music.

Another way to present your magic is by using it to teach. This is what I do most of the time. Here's an example.

In one of my school assembly shows, named The No Bully Zone, I talk to kids about bullying, why it's not a good thing to do, what to do if you are getting picked on, and more.

For one of my routines, I wanted to talk to the audience about empathy. Empathy is the idea of thinking about, or imagining, how someone else feels, and letting that person know.

This was a really hard idea to put with a magic trick, and I thought about what kind of magic trick I could use to illustrate empathy.

The trick I chose to use is one where I draw a picture of one of my volunteers on a dry erase board. I show it to the audience, and everyone laughs because I am not a very good artist. Then I take a second dry erase board and ask that same volunteer to draw a picture of me! What the audience does not realize is that while she is drawing me, I'm whispering to her and telling her to make the drawing of me look really silly, like giving me a tail, and other fun things.

Then each dry erase board is put into an envelope. The volunteer holds her envelope with her drawing in it on one side of the stage. I hold my drawing I made in the other envelope on the other side of the stage.

I talk to the audience about empathy, explain what it is, and tell everyone that empathy is imagining yourself in the other person's position... and then the volunteer and I both open our envelopes and show the audience that the drawings have changed places!

So in that case, the 'presentation' was teaching everyone what a certain word meant.

Another way of presenting magic is with poems. In one of my school assemblies, I use a rhyming poem with a magic trick to tell the story of *The Cat in the Hat Comes Back*, by Dr. Seuss.

Some magicians tell jokes while they perform. They might start a trick, such as having an audience member pick a playing card from a deck, then tell some jokes, then do another step in the trick, tell some more jokes, and finish the trick.

Personally, I don't like that way of presenting magic because when magicians perform that way, it seems like the magic is not very important. That doesn't mean that I am right, it just means that's how I feel.

As you can see, there are many ways to present your magic. The cool thing is that you can use different ways of presenting magic in the same show! That's what I do: In many of my school assemblies, I might start off the show with a trick set to music, do some tricks where I am teaching something and using magic to help explain these things, and maybe end the show with another trick set to music.

Secret #10 - Prepare!

When it comes to everything in life, people who do the best are prepared. For magic, that means making sure everything is right before you perform magic.

What kinds of things do you need to prepare for in magic? Here's just a few things:

☺ Making sure all of your props are in the right place so you can reach them easily while you are performing.

☺ Before the show, look over everything and check that nothing is broken or missing

☺ You've practiced your moves so your magic looks really good

☺ You have rehearsed your presentation so when you speak, your words are really smooth

When you are prepared, it means that not only are you ready for the show itself, but also for anything that might go wrong during the show.

Since this book is mostly about performing magic over the Internet, you also want to prepare by doing a few more things:

☺ Check to make sure you have good lighting when you do your magic

☺ Make sure that your computer or tablet is set up at the right height so your audience can see your magic clearly

☺ Make sure your computer or tablet is set up in the right place so your audience will not see anything that would give away the secret when you perform your magic.

Being prepared means that you also think about what could go wrong and what you will say or do if something does goes wrong.

This is important: Being prepared in case something goes wrong does not mean you are being negative and trying to make something bad happen. It simply means that you are ready just in case.

The idea of planning for something to go wrong reminds me of when I was in high school and I was late to school a bunch of times.

I set my alarm clock at a certain time, and when I got up and left for school, if nothing went wrong, I would be on time… but if I ran into a problem, I'd be late.

Some of the things that would delay me were: having trouble crossing the street because of a lot of traffic, my baby brother hiding my shoes on me, my mother reminding me to take out the garbage that I had forgotten to do the night before, or if I forgot something when I left my house (like my homework) and then had to turn around and go back to my house to get whatever it was that I forgot.

All of these things that I had not planned for would cause me to be late.

After I explained to my teachers why I was late and how it wasn't my fault, they would each say, "Well, you should have planned for those things and gotten up earlier."

At the time, when I was a teenager in high school, the idea of planning for things to go wrong seemed very strange to me.

Now, as a grownup, I know how important it is to plan for things to go wrong. It's not about having negative thoughts. It's just knowing that weird things will happen, so it's best to be prepared.

These days, when I drive to a show, I will look at my GPS on my car. If it tells me it will take me 20 minutes to get to my shows, I will give myself 30-35 minutes just in case.

Being prepared is how you become not only a master magician, but also a master at lifNow, onto learning some fun magic!

Chapter 4:
Magic Using Stuff from
Around Your House

This chapter has some really fun magic in it that is easy to do, fun, and amazing. Like the title says, it uses stuff you can probably find around your house. Really, just about everything in this book uses stuff you can find around your house, but the tricks in all the other chapters fit nicely into categories: money, string, cards, and so on.

On the other hand, this first chapter involves random stuff, like paperclips, a rubber band, and so on. So, this chapter is kind of a hodge-podge of tricks. But I didn't really want the first chapter to read as 'A Hodge-Podge of Tricks.'

Anyway, let's get to the first trick!

Trick #1: The Invisible Ball

What the trick looks like to the audience: The great magician named Beth The Spectacular shows her audience a brown paper bag, the kind that many people use to carry their lunches in.

She explains, "I have something really special in this bag, I have to take very good care of it because I don't want to lose it. Would you like to see it?"

The audience says yes!

Beth reaches into the bag with her hand and pulls out... nothing! It looks like her hand is empty, even though she has her fingers curled in such a way that it almost looks like she's holding an invisible ball!

Beth smiles at the audience says, "I know what you are thinking: 'Beth's just being silly! There's no ball!' But there is—watch!"

Beth pretends to toss the invisible ball into the air and catches it. As she catches the ball, her hands drops as though the weight of the ball was pushing her hand down. She pretends to toss the ball even higher and catches it in the paper bag. When the 'ball' lands in the paper bag, the audience hears a 'thwack' sound of something landing in the bag!

What you need for this trick: The only thing you need for this trick is a paper bag and your own two hands!

The secret to the trick: There are two basic secrets to this trick. The first secret is to make the 'thwack' sound of something solid landing in the bag, you are really flicking your fingers in the back of the bag! The second secret is acting! Let me explain both in the next section.

How to perform the trick: There are a lot of versions of this trick in other magic trick books, and every version I have seen talks about holding the bag by the opening with your first and second fingers on the outside and your thumb on the inside. Then, to make the noise, the books tell you to snap your fingers the same way you would snap your fingers... well, the same way you would snap your fingers if you weren't holding the bag!

For me, this did not work very well. I sometimes wonder if the people who write other magic books really understand how to write things so people understand them.

So for this trick, I came up with my own way of doing it that was easier for me and easier for the kids I teach this trick to.

The way I do it, I'm holding the bag by the opening. I'm using my right hand. My first two fingers are in the opening of the bag. My thumb of the same hand is on the outside of the bag. All three fingers are pushed together to keep the bag from falling to the ground.

When I want to make the 'thwack' sound, I flick my thumb across my first two fingers in the bag. Just a quick flick—it's kind of like if you've ever had a little tiny ball of rubber cement stuck to your fingers after you have used rubber cement, and you use your thumb on the same hand to kind of flick that little ball off of your fingers.

It's the same kind of motion. Since your first two fingers are on the inside of the bag and your thumb is on the outside of the bag, when you go to flick your thumb across your other fingers, your thumb is really flicking the paper of the bag... so it makes that 'something-solid-just-landed-inside-this-bag-even-though-I can't-see-it' sound.

So that's the first part of the secret (remember, I said there were two parts).

Let's now talk about the second part of the secret: Acting!

This is really important. You have to act (or 'pretend') that you are really tossing that ball in the air. You have to pretend you can feel the weight of the ball in your hand. You have to pretend you can feel the solid shape of the ball in your hand... remember how in the story it looked like Beth's fingers were wrapped around something solid? That's important too.

If you just let your hand that's holding the bag dangle at your side, and using your other hand you just kind of make a throwing motion at the bag, no one is going to think that this is a really good magic trick.

To make this trick look really good, you can take a real ball and actually toss it in the air and catch it in the bag. Record yourself doing that. Then watch how your hands move when using the real ball. Then remember how the real ball felt: How it felt in your hand when you were holding it, how it felt to feel it land in the bag, and how it felt to feel the weight of the ball inside the bag.

Work on your timing, so when you pretend to toss that invisible ball, when it is supposed to land in the bag, THAT is when you make the 'ball landing in the paper bag' sound. If you do it too soon or too late, then the trick won't look right.

And you can use your eyes!

Look at your hand as you pretend to hold the invisible ball... pretend to follow the ball with your eyes as you toss it up in the air... and pretend to follow the ball with your eyes as you catch the ball in the bag.

This is a really fun trick to start this book with because every great magician becomes a great actor!

Remember, at the end of the chapter, I'll list the website your mom or dad can visit to let you watch videos of me performing and explaining every trick in this book!

Trick #2: The Linking Paperclips

What the trick looks like to the audience: Magician Curt The Magnificent tells his audience, "There is a classic magic trick called 'The Linking Rings.' It involves big metal rings linking and unlinking and looks really neat. There's a way to do it with something you have all seen: paperclips!"

Curt takes out a slip of paper about the size of a dollar bill along with two paperclips. He folds the paper in two places so that if you were to look down at the top of the folded paper, it would look like a letter 'z.'

He then takes the paperclips and places them onto the paper, clipping the ends of the 'z' together in such a way that the clips are separate from each other.

"This happens really quickly, so watch carefully!" Curt says. He then pulls the ends of the paper away from each other very quickly. Both paperclips pop off the paper and are now linked!

What you need for this trick: You'll need one piece of paper that is about the size of a dollar bill...or you can just use a dollar bill. You'll also need two paperclips. You can use any kind you can find in your house, but since this book is about doing magic over the internet, you might want to try to find some of those bright neon-colored paperclips.

The secret to the trick: The paperclips are put on the folds of the paper in such a way that when you pull the ends, the paperclips are pushed together and automatically link.

How to perform the trick: This is one of those tricks that magicians call "self-working," because it doesn't require any real skill to perform. Because of that, this trick is a great opportunity to work on what you are going to say when performing the trick. A great magician looks at a self-working trick as an opportunity to do great magic and takes extra care to make sure that the trick is not just a trick, but is very entertaining.

To put the paperclips on the paper correctly, first fold the paper into the shape of a 'z.' Then, place the paperclips onto the paper in the following way.

For paperclips to do their job, they have to be clipped to at least two pieces of paper. Each of the two paperclips in this trick are going to be clipped to two layers of the same paper—that's why the paper is folded into a 'z' shape.

If you look at the 'z' fold in your paper, you'll see that it has three parts to it. The 'z' has one straight line at the top, one straight line at the bottom, and a diagonal line in the middle. You are going to take one paperclip and clip the top straight line together with the top of the diagonal line. Then you are going to clip the second paperclip to the bottom straight line together with the bottom of the diagonal line.

When you are ready to make the paperclips link, you can pull the two ends away from each other. The paperclips are forced together, and they link automatically.

I should also mention that out of all of the tricks in this book, this is one of the tricks I wanted to teach that made me wish I could draw pictures. It's also one of the tricks that made me realize that giving my readers access to videos of the tricks would really help!

Be sure to get your parents to go to the website at the end of this chapter so that you can see this trick in action. This will help you a great deal if you are having trouble with this trick.

Trick #3: The Jumping Rubber Band

What the trick looks like to the audience: Dora The Amazing offers to show her audience something amazing with a rubber band.

"Has anyone here ever seen Star Trek? I always thought it was so cool that the people on the starship could transport all the way from space onto a planet in just a few seconds! I am going to cause this rubber band to transport in an instant!"

Dora holds up the rubber band in her left hand and flashes the front and back of her right hand to show there is nothing else that she is using for the trick.

She wraps the rubber band around her first two fingers on her right hand and again shows both sides of her right hand. Using her left hand, she pulls the rubber band tight and curls her right fingers into a fist.

"On the count of three," Dora says, "you will see the rubber band instantly jump from around my first two fingers to my third and fourth fingers. Watch closely! One... two... three!"

As Dora says "three," she unfolds her curled righthand fingers. In a blink of an eye, the rubber band has jumped from being wrapped around her first two fingers to being wrapped around her third and fourth fingers!

What you need for this trick: You'll need one rubber band. The brighter the color, the better! You will also need your two hands. That's it!

The secret to the trick: In addition to the rubber band being wrapped around the first two fingers, the rubber band is also secretly wrapped around all four of your fingertips in such a way that when you unfold your curled fingers, the rubber band jumps from your first two fingers to your third and fourth fingers.

How to perform the trick: This trick is pretty easy to perform but it does involve one secret move you need to keep hidden from your audience.

The rubber band you use should be a regular rubber band, the kind that people use all the time. There are big thick rubber bands that grocery stores use to hold vegetables together, really huge rubber bands that some people use to exercise, and little, iddy-biddy rubber bands that dentists use. You want a regular rubber band that is easy to find around the house.

I'm going to describe the directions for a right-handed person, in other words, the rubber band will be wrapped around the right hand. If you are left-handed, you can easily do the exact same trick with your left hand.

Take the rubber band and wrap it around your first two fingers on your right hand. The rubber band will probably be loose around your fingers so you can just drop the rubber band around your first two fingers. Let the rubber band rest at the base of your fingers, where your fingers connect to the rest of your hand.

Turn your right hand so the back of your hand is facing away from you. This is what your audience will see when you make the rubber band jump. With the palm of your right hand facing you, use your left hand to pull on the rubber band and stretch it enough so that when you curl your right fingers into a fist, your right fingertips all go into the rubber band. Then let go of the rubber band.

Look at your hand now. If you did it correctly, your right fingertips should now have the rubber band wrapped around them, but from the other side of your hand, it looks like the rubber band is still just wrapped around your first two fingers. If you need to adjust your right fingertips so the rubber band is in the right place, that's okay.

Also, if you have really little fingers, you might find the rubber band is not tight enough and won't stay around your fingertips. If this is the case, when you first start the trick and wrap the rubber band around your first two fingers, you can double up the rubber band... in other words, wrap it around your first two fingers twice.

When you have the rubber band set up correctly—the audience sees the back of your hand and the rubber band wrapped around your first two fingers, and you can look at your fingers curled into a fist and see the rubber band wrapped around your fingertips—you are ready to make the rubber band jump!

Quickly uncurl your right fingers. The band will quickly jump from your first two fingers to your third and fourth fingers. This part works all by itself!

Here's a few important things to remember:

1. You want to be sure that right before you uncurl your right fingers, the rubber band is wrapped around your fingertips in the right place... the rubber band should be resting just above your fingernails.
2. The secret move is when you use your other hand to pull the rubber band away from your palm, so that when you curl your fingers into a fist, your fingertips are able to go into the rubber band. You must keep your hand's palm facing you while you do this.
3. The audience will see you tugging on the rubber band, but they won't really know what you are doing. You can cover this action by asking the audience a question, such as, "Have you ever seen a magic trick with a rubber band before?" or you can say something kind of funny to get everyone to laugh such as: "Boy, if this rubber band was any

tighter, I think my fingers would turn purple and fall off!"

4. Getting people to laugh is great misdirection!

5. You can do the same trick but start off by wrapping the rubber band around your third and fourth fingers. Then after you do the secret move, the rubber band will jump to your first two fingers!

6. Since this book is about doing magic over the internet, try to use a brightly colored rubber band so everyone watching will be able to clearly see what is happening.

Website:

Ask your parents to go to www.VirtualMagicBook.com and enter their name to get you access to the videos for the tricks in this chapter. It's important to ask your parents to do this for you to stay safe online!

Chapter 5:
Rope & String Magic

This chapter has some amazing magic that will look great over the internet! Tricks with string and rope are so popular because there's so much magic you can do with string and rope—almost as many tricks as card magic!

One BIG word of warning: Some tricks in this chapter use scissors to cut a straw, string, even rope. Depending on how you want to prepare the tricks, there might also be another sharp object involved. If you are going to use scissors or anything sharp, it is best to have your mom or dad with you to stay safe! You should also use safety scissors whenever possible.

I know you might be thinking, "I am old enough to use scissors without hurting myself," and you might be right. My job as a teacher of magic is to always remind you to be careful. Even as a grownup, I have made mistakes with scissors when I was doing magic because I wasn't paying enough attention, and I have hurt myself.

So, have fun, but be safe!

Trick #1: Two-To-One String Trick

This is one of my favorite tricks in this entire book! I still remember the first time I saw someone perform this—it fooled me so perfectly!

What the trick looks like to the audience: Ernie The Mystifying Magician asks his audience if they want to see something impossible!

He holds up two strings in his right hand. The strings are completely separate from each other. The audience can clearly see both ends of each piece of string.

Ernie explains, "There was once a little boy who was trapped in a well. His friends offered to lower a rope to help pull him out to safety. There was a problem, though. Each rope was too short."

Ernie points to the ropes. "One of the friends had the idea to tie two of the ropes together. Another friend said, 'but if the knot comes undone, the boy could fall!'

Another friend said, 'What if there was a way to join these two ropes together without using a knot?'"

Then, using his right hand, Ernie places the ends of the two strings into his left hand and closes his fingers around the two ends. Using his right hand, he pulls one of the ends slowly out of his left hand. He reveals that the two pieces of string have now magically become one long string!

What you need for this trick: You'll need some yarn and a pair of safety scissors.

The secret to the trick: There is actually only one piece of string used the whole time!

The reason why this trick uses yarn and not thread or other kinds of string is because yarn is actually made up of several thinner pieces of very soft string that are sort of twirled together.

From about half of the way down the length of the yarn, two little 'rabbit ear' ends are created. Your fingers hold the piece of string by covering where the rabbit ears come from. When you put the string in your other hand and pull one of the ends of the string, those 'ears' get pulled back into the string, so it looks like one long piece of string again.

How to perform the trick: To get ready for the trick, using your safety scissors, cut off a piece of yarn about 12 inches long.

Once the yarn is cut, lay the piece of yarn on a table. Measure about halfway down the length of the string from either one of the ends. Using your fingers, start tugging at the string at that 'one-half of the length' spot.

Tug on the yarn until you start to get two pieces sticking out. Earlier I called them 'rabbit ears' because to me they sort of look like little rabbit ears! Really, though, you are simply gently pulling on that section of the string until you get two parts of the string sticking out.

Keep pulling until the 'rabbit ears; are about an inch long each. Then, because the 'ears' are kind of unraveled, you'll need to twist each end until these ends look just like the string did originally.

If you have done this right, then you'll have a piece of string with two 'ends' sticking out about one-half of the length of the string. It's sort of like a couple of very short branches growing out of a tree trunk!

To do the trick, keep the string hidden until you are ready to show everyone. Hold the string between your first finger and thumb. You want to hold the string so your finger and thumb cover the spot where the two little 'ears' come out. Hold the string doubled over, so the longer two halves of the string are dangling below your thumb and first finger, and above your first finger and thumb, those two little ears stick straight up.

When you do it correctly, it looks just like you are holding two separate pieces of string!

To create the magic effect of two strings becoming one, put the middle of the string (where the two 'ears' are sticking out) into your left hand. Don't let go of the string with your right finger and thumb until the middle of the string is completely in your left hand. As you let go with your right fingers, close your left fingers completely around the middle of the string. This prevents your audience from seeing that it is really just one string.

With your left hand closed, show your audience what looks like two pieces of string sticking out of your fist. Then, using your right fingers, pull one end of the string out of your left hand. As you pull with your right fingers, it's really important to keep squeezing your left hand closed. This helps to draw those little 'ears' back into the middle of the yarn.

You can show the two strings have joined into one string by holding one end of the string in your left hand by the left thumb and first finger, and holding the other end with your right thumb and first finger.

Since the middle of the string where the two 'ears' were pulled out might still be kind of loose, pull the string tight between your two hands, which will help keep that middle from looking kind of loose or floppy, and prevent anyone from figuring out the secret.

Another professional tip for this trick is for you to wear a dark, solid shirt. Don't wear a shirt that is bright or has a crazy kind of pattern because it might be harder for some people to see the string against a 'busy' background like that.

When I do the trick, I also use a brightly colored yarn, like yellow, white, or pink. The bright color of the yarn will show up better against a dark shirt when doing this trick over the internet.

Trick #2: Cut and Restored String

What the trick looks like to the audience: Magician Fran the Conjurer holds up a drinking straw and a piece of string to her audience.

She says, "I have this friend who breaks stuff all the time! He keeps calling me and saying, 'can you help me? I broke something! Can you fix it with your magic?'"

Fran takes the piece of string and slides it down the straw until the ends of the string are sticking out of both sides of the straw.

"Yesterday," she says, 'I snapped a string in half! My mom uses this string to hang something in our bathroom! Can you help me?'"

As Fran is telling the story, she cuts the straw and string in half, ruining both!

"So, I decided to use my magic to help him, because when you are a good friend, you help out!"

Fran separates the two cut pieces of straw... to reveal that the string has become completely whole again!

What you need for this trick: You'll need one drinking straw every time you do the trick. The straw really does get cut in half by the scissors, so every time you do this, you ruin a straw!

You also need one piece of string. The string never actually gets cut, so you can use the same piece of string every time you do the trick.

You also need a pair of scissors to cut the straw during the trick.

The secret to the trick: This trick works because the straw is prepared in a secret way that makes it so when you cut the straw, you ONLY cut the straw, not the string.

How to perform the trick: The most important part of this trick has to be done before you perform the trick.

For this part of the preparation, you absolutely need a grownup to help you to make sure you don't get hurt!

Have your mom or dad take a very sharp cutting utensil and cut a two-inch long slit in the middle of the straw. In the past, I have also done this using scissors, but the problem with doing it that way is that cutting the straw with scissors actually removes part of the straw, so the audience watching the trick might notice that part of the straw is missing.

Using a very sharp blade means there is a slit in the straw, but nothing has actually been removed, so the shape of the straw will hold it in place and hide the slit.

To see how the slit keeps the string from being cut while the straw is cut, drop one end of the string into the straw and let that end come of the other end of the straw. You will want to use a piece of string that is at least a few inches longer than the entire straw. This is so your audience can see the string coming out of both ends of the straw.

Once you have the string in the straw, bend the straw completely in half in the middle, right where the slit is. You can then pull both ends of the string. Now let the bent straw unbend a tiny little bit. You should see the middle of the string coming out of the slit. This part of the string will be below where the actual bend is in the straw.

When you do the trick, you will bend the straw completely in half, then pull on both ends of the string (which pulls the middle of the string out of the slit and away from the bent middle of the straw), and using your scissors, cut just the bent part of the straw, which cuts the straw in half, but not the string.

This looks really good and impossible!

Try to use a piece of yarn if you can get it to go into the straw. Yarn is very thick and will look good on your webcam. Also, try to use a piece of yarn that is a different color than the straw so when your audience watches the trick, they can tell the yarn apart from the straw.

Trick #3: Two Ropes Into One

This trick not only looks great when you are showing magic to friends over the internet, but it also is great when you are doing magic for a big group of people watching magic live, in person!

What the trick looks like to the audience: Girty The Magnificent tells her audience she is going to walk her dog, but she needs a longer dog leash. She holds up two pieces of rope in her left hand.

"I don't think either of these pieces of rope will be long enough to walk my dog," Girty says. "Let's see if magic can help!"

Girty ties the two ropes together... then waves her right hand over the knot while saying some magic words. She then tugs on the knot... which slides all the way off of the rope, revealing that the two ropes have now magically become one!

What you need for this trick: You'll need either two pieces of rope or two pieces of yarn, depending on how 'big' you want the trick to be. I usually use rope, but that is because when I do magic, I am usually in front of hundreds of people. If you are doing this over the internet, using yarn will look great too.

If you do decide to use rope, try to find very soft rope that bends easily. Some rope, like the kind that people use for hanging clothes outside, are way too stiff for this trick. A craft store like Joann Fabrics usually has something softer that will work.

The secret to the trick: There really are two pieces of rope, but one rope is very long, about two feet, while the other piece of rope is about six inches. The long piece of rope is folded in half. The short piece of rope is also folded in half.

Let the long rope drape in half over your arm. Take the short rope and tuck one end under the middle of the long rope. Now lift both ends of the short rope. The long rope dangles with its ends pointing down toward the ground.

Now hold the place where the two ropes meet in your left hand. With the ends of the short rope poking up through the top of your left fist and the ends of the long rope poking down through the bottom of your left fist, you now look like you are holding two separate pieces of rope that are about a foot long each.

How to perform the trick: Just like you did with the first trick in this chapter, you are going to keep everything out of site of your audience before you do the trick.

When it is time to perform, you will hold up the ropes in your left hand with the ends sticking out of your fist just like I explained in the 'secret to the trick.'

To do the trick, you need to tie the two ends poking out of the top of your left hand into a knot. To the audience, it looks like you are tying two ropes together into a knot.

What you are really doing is typing one rope, the short rope, into a knot around the middle of the long knot.

Once the knot is tied, you can hold the rope between your two hands by the ends. It looks to your audience like you are holding two one-foot ropes tied together. Then you can slowly and carefully slide the knot down the length of the rope and finally right off the end of the long rope. This looks very surprising!

The hard part is to do the knot tying so that it looks natural... without letting anyone watching in on the secret.

While this trick is very easy, if you want to make sure it looks really good to your audience, do this: Take two actual one-foot pieces of rope, hold them in your left hand, and then practice tying them together while watching yourself in a mirror and then recording yourself.

When you are doing the trick for real, you are tying that short rope into a knot, and you are trying to keep your audience from seeing too much so they don't see what is really going on.

By practicing first by really tying two one-foot pieces of rope together, you will learn the right hand and finger movements to make everything look the right way!

Website:

Ask your parents to go to www.VirtualMagicBook.com and enter their name to get you access to the videos for the tricks in this chapter. It's important to ask your parents to do this for you to stay safe online!

The next chapter has really fun magic with money! Everyone knows how important money is in life, so by doing magic with money, your audience will be very interested!

Chapter 6:
Money Magic

Doing magic with money is always popular. In this chapter, you will learn how to make it look as though you are creating money by magic, making money float in the air, and making money disappear!

Trick #1: Multiplying Money

To me, this trick is just about perfect! When you start practicing this in front of a mirror, you will think this looks like real magic! It's an awesome trick to do over the internet, too!

What the trick looks like to the audience: Harry the Awesome shows his audience a dime in his left hand.

"I'm saving my money to buy my mom a nice birthday present. Sometimes I can use magic to save money even faster!"

Harry shows his right hand empty, then reaches over to his left hand where the dime is. Taking the dime in his right fingers... Harry suddenly shows that instead of one dime, he is now holding two quarters, one in each hand!

What you need for this trick: You'll need two U.S. quarters, one U.S. dime, and your two hands! If you live outside of the United States, you can use two large coins and one small coin of your country's currency. As long as the big coins fit in your hand in a certain way, you can use any coins.

You can also use a penny for your small coin if you'd like. Then, when your audience sees the two quarters, they will also be surprised by the color change of the penny to the quarters.

For me, I like using a dime because it's such a teeny-tiny coin that it makes the magical appearance of the two quarters even more surprising!

The secret to the trick: The dime actually hides the two quarters from the audience's view!

How to perform the trick: Take the two quarters and stack them on top of each other. Then take those two quarters and, using your left hand, kind of wrap your first finger and thumb around the stacked edges of those two coins.

While holding the coins in place like that, if you turn your left hand so your first fingertip and thumbtip face you, you will see that looking at the quarters in that position means you only have to hide the edges of the quarters from view! That's where the dime comes in.

Take the dime and place it right between your first finger and thumb so that you can see the face of the dime. Let your other three fingers spread open wide. If you look at the dime "head on," it looks like your hand is only holding that little tiny dime and the rest of your hand is totally empty!

You cannot let anyone look "down" on your hand, otherwise they will see the two quarters stacked on top of each other. That is what makes this trick so perfect for the internet: You can hold your hand as close as you possibly can to your computer or tablet's webcam and as long as you hold the dime so that your audience is looking at the face of the dime, there is nothing to see to give away the trick!

To turn the dime into the two quarters, show your right hand empty, front and back, and cover the dime with your right four fingers. While the dime is hidden from your audience's view, slide the dime on top of the two quarters, turn your left hand so the faces of the quarters will be facing your audience, and using your right hand, take away the top quarter (with the dime hidden behind it), showing both quarters to your audience.

I love this trick! This is one of my favorite money tricks ever!

Trick #2: Floating Dollar Bill

What the trick looks like to the audience: Indigo the Great holds up a dollar bill for his audience to see.

As he begins folding it, he says, "The weirdest thing happened to me the other day! I had this dream I became a superhero! I could fly around and stuff, it was awesome! When I woke up, I couldn't fly in real life, but I could make something float in the air. Check this out!"

After Indigo finishes folding the edges of the dollar bill, he carefully sets one end of the dollar on his thumb... and lets go, leaving the rest of the dollar suspended in the air! He moves her hand with the dollar bill up close to the camera of his computer so the audience can see that there are no strings or anything holding the bill up!

What you need for this trick: You'll need a one-dollar bill and a quarter. Try to get a dollar bill that is sort of new so it will hold its shape when you begin folding it. An old dollar bill that is kind of floppy does not work as well.

If you are outside of the United States, you can use any paper money as long as you can fold it and it will hold its shape. I say that because some countries use "paper money" that has plastic in it and might not fold as well. Any coin that can be hidden by the paper money will work too, although I am not sure that a really small coin like a dime or penny is heavy enough for the trick to work.

The secret to the trick: The dollar bill's edges are folded in such a way as to keep the quarter hidden at one end of the bill. The end of the bill with the quarter hidden is placed over your thumb tip. The weight of the quarter keeps the rest of the dollar bill from falling off of your thumb. Because your audience does not know about the quarter holding the bill in place, it looks like the bill is floating!

How to perform the trick: To do the trick, you'll need to prepare the dollar by folding it. Put the dollar "George side down" on a table. With President Washington's head face down on the table, you'll see the big word 'ONE' in the middle of the bill. Fold the long edges of the bill in about a half an inch on both sides. Do the same thing with the short edges. Press down on the creases to make sure when you fold them during the performance, they will fold easily and hold their place. Unfold the bill, and you are ready to perform!

Hold the bill in your right hand with your right fingers in front and your thumb in the back with George facing your webcam. Your right thumb is also holding the quarter against the back of the bill.

When I have taught this trick in my Discover Magic online magic classes, some kids worry that their thumbs are smaller than the quarter. That does not matter because the dollar will hide the quarter.

As you start to tell your story (remember, you can create your own story if you want!), start folding the edges of the dollar bill again, right along the creases you made earlier. The important thing to practice here is to make these folds while still keeping the quarter hidden... without it looking like you are hiding anything.

Making the dollar float is the easy part. The part that needs a lot of practice is folding the edges of the bill.

Once you have all four edges of the bill folded, if you like, you can hold the folded bill by the end without the coin...and carefully let the end holding the coin hang downwards. The creased, folded edges of the bill will hold the quarter in place.

This is really good magic because when you let that end of the bill dangle, the audience thinks there is nothing "tricky" with the bill... and you don't have to say anything!

Turn your left-hand thumb up so your thumbnail is facing the ground while the pad of your thumb is facing the sky. This is where the quarter is going to go.

Carefully set the end of the bill with the hidden quarter on top of your thumb. It will take you some practice to get used to balancing the quarter and bill so everything stays in position.

When you let go of the bill, let go very slowly, as this helps make the floating look more surprising and mysterious!

Wave your other hand above and below the floating bill and bring the bill in very close to the webcam so everyone can see that there are no threads or string holding the bill up!

Be careful to never show the trick in a position where people can watch while looking down on the bill because they might see the quarter between the folded edges of the bill!

Trick #3: The Disappearing Coin

What the trick looks like to the audience: Jane The Mysterious shows her audience a coin and sets it on a table on top of a piece of construction paper or napkin.

"I have a problem," she says. On the table next to the coin, there is a clear drinking glass sitting mouth down. Jane wraps the clear glass with a dark napkin. She places both over the coin, waves her hands dramatically, and lifts the napkin off of the glass.

The audience can clearly see through the drinking glass to the table: The coin has disappeared!

"My problem is I keep making money disappear," Jane says. "But it's okay. I can make it come back! Watch!"

Jane covers the glass with the napkin again. This time, she waves a magic wand, then lifts the napkin-covered glass... and reveals that the coin has returned!

What you need for this trick: To make the coin disappear, you will need:

- a coin
- two paper napkins that are the same color (you can also use pieces of colored construction paper)
- a different colored napkin that is a darker color
- a clear drinking glass
- scissors
- rubber cement.

The secret to the trick: A paper napkin is spread out on the table. The glass has a piece of a second paper napkin (that is the exact same color set on the table) cut into a circle and glued to the mouth (or opening) of the glass. When the glass is set mouth down over the coin on the paper napkin, it looks like the coin has disappeared because the napkin glued to the glass blends in with the napkin on the table!

How to perform the trick: When you get two paper napkins that match, make sure that the napkins have a solid color and pattern to them. If there are decoration lines in the pattern, or circles, or anything like that, when you put the glass down, if the lines or circles, or whatever decorations on the napkin do not line up, members of your audience might figure out what is going on.

It's best to use plain colored napkins. To get one of the napkins glued to the top of the glass, you can do it a couple of different ways:

- Spread one of the napkins out on a table. Put a REALLY thin line of rubber cement along the mouth edge of the glass. Set the mouth down on the napkin. Do not move the glass or napkin at all for at least an hour, giving the rubber cement time to dry completely. Then carefully cut away the rest of the paper from the outside of the mouth of the glass.

- The second way is to trace the mouth of the glass on the paper, cut the circle out, and then glue the round piece of paper to the mouth of the glass.

I have tried it both ways. You can try both and see which way is easier for you. No matter which way you do it, you have to make sure that the circle covering the mouth of the glass is cut perfectly so no one watching the trick can see any edges that will reveal how the trick is done.

I also listed you can do this with construction paper instead of napkins. I think the trick looks better with napkins, because people watching your show would see a napkin on a table and think that it makes sense.

If people see a piece of construction paper laying on a table, they might think, "Hey, why is there a piece of construction paper laying on the table? That looks kind of weird."

But construction paper does not tear as easily as a paper napkin, so it is a lot easier to cut and get the circle into exactly the right shape.

You can try both kinds of paper and see which one you like better.

When you do the trick, make sure your webcam is aimed at the table so everyone can see the table clearly. Set the coin in the center of the napkin. Then cover the glass with the different colored napkin before you lift the glass.

Set the napkin-covered glass on top of the coin. When you take away the napkin that is wrapped around the clear glass, everyone will be able to see through the side of the glass, see the top of the table, and think the coin has disappeared because it's covered by the secret circle of paper (or napkin) on the glass.

To make the coin come back, wrap the glass again with the different colored napkin and take the glass away. The coin has reappeared!

Website:

Ask your parents to go to www.VirtualMagicBook.com and enter their name to get you access to the videos for the tricks in this chapter. It's important to ask your parents to do this for you to stay safe online!

Chapter 7:
Card Tricks

These tricks are really awesome card tricks that are fun, easy to do, and amazing! In fact, I do one of these tricks when I do one of my big shows in front of 400-500 kids!

Trick #1: The Fetch Cards

What the trick looks like to the audience: The Amazing Karen takes a deck of cards and sets them on the table. She then holds up the four Jacks in a fan so the audience can see all four faces.

"My cards are kind of like my dog: They come when I call them," Karen says. She lays the four Jacks face down on top of the deck and squares up all of the cards.

Karen looks at one of the people watching her show on Zoom. "Okay, you get to name one of the cards! I'm putting this Jack into the middle of the deck. What do you want to name him?"

As Karen is talking, the audience can watch her lift the top card off the top of the deck and push it into the middle of the deck. Karen is very careful to let everyone see that the card really is going into the middle of the deck.

Her volunteer says, "Let's call him Frodo!"

"Frodo it is," Karen laughs. She repeats this with three more volunteers, asking these three people to each name one of the remaining three Jacks on top of the deck of cards. As each Jack is named, each is pushed into the middle of the deck of cards.

The three remaining Jacks were named Molly, Sophie, and Stanlee.

"All right," Karen says, "when I count to three, we will all call out, 'come here, Frodo, come here Molly, come here Sophie, come here Stanlee!"

Karen counts to three and everyone calls out the four names. This gets everyone involved and is a lot of silly fun!

Karen says, "My cards are really good because they come when they hear their names!" Karen reaches down to the deck and turns over the top four cards. It's the Jacks! They all magically returned to the top of the deck!

What you need for this trick: You'll need a regular deck of cards and your two hands. That's it!

The secret to the trick: Behind the fan of the four Jacks, there is a hidden stack of four other cards. The audience does not know about these other four cards. When the four Jacks are shown and placed on top of the deck, you have really added eight cards instead of four. As you take the top four cards off of the top of the deck and push them into the middle of the deck, the audience thinks it's the Jacks, but it's really just those four other cards!

After the four other cards are pushed into the middle of the deck, the four cards on top of the deck are now the four Jacks, so you are then ready to show the four Jacks have "magically" returned to the top of the deck!

How to perform the trick: Take out the four Jacks from your deck of cards. If your deck of cards does not have all four Jacks, you can use the four Queens, four Aces, four Sixes... as long as you have four of the same cards.

Spread the four same cards face down on your table in a little fan, so all four cards are touching each other, and you can see all four cards. Then take any other four cards out of the deck. These four other cards can be any cards at all. Stack all four cards on top of each other face down. Then put these cards down on top of the face down Jacks (or whatever four cards you are using).

When you do the trick, you will need to pick up the cards from the table and hold all eight cards facing your webcam so that the four Jacks are in that little fan and the other four cards are hidden behind those four Jacks. Never show anyone the backs!

Square up all four eight cards and lay them face down on the deck. Take the top four cards off of the top of the deck and push them into the middle of the deck one at a time. As you take these four cards off the top of the deck, make sure you hold the cards in such a way that no one watching can see the faces of those cards, because these will be those four other cards, not your four Jacks.

After you talk about the cards coming back when you call them, take the top four cards off the top of the deck one at a time, and show that the Jacks have magically returned to the top of the deck!

Make sure you practice all of these moves in front of a mirror and then record yourself so you can make sure that you never let anyone see anything that would reveal the secret of the trick.

What I really like about this trick is that it gets people involved in the trick: You are asking people questions, and people are giving you names for the cards.

Remember, when you get other people involved with your magic, they will enjoy it much more!

Trick #2: 2-Card Monte

What the trick looks like to the audience: Larry the Wise tells his audience, "I'm going to turn one of YOU into the magician!"

Larry holds up a paper bag.

He says, "I'm going to drop two cards into this bag," and he drops two cards, stacked on top of each other, face down into the bag. He reaches back in and removes one card and shows its face to the audience.

"I'm sorry, I need to show you what two cards I am using! This is the Six of Hearts..." he puts the Six back into the bag and takes the other card out and shows it's face to the audience. "The second card is the Three of Spades," he says, as he puts that card back into the bag.

As he starts shaking the bag, Larry continues, "I'm going to shake up the bag so I don't know which card is which, and then I will take one of the cards out of the bag, and you are going to guess correctly which card is still in the bag."

Larry stops shaking the bag and reaches in and removes one card, showing it's back to the audience. He asks one of the people watching to guess which card is still in the bag.

"The Three of Spades!" the volunteer says.

Larry reaches into the bag and removes the other card, showing it to be the Three of Spades. Indigo puts the Three of Spades on top of the other card and shows the bag empty—there were only two cards in the bag.

Larry repeats the trick, and each time, someone from the audience is able to guess which card is left in the bag each time.

What you need for this trick: You'll need two playing cards that are very different from each other. In the story, Larry used a red Six of Hearts and a black Three of Spades. These were really great cards to use because as soon as the audience sees one of the cards, they know right away which card is which. If Larry had used the Two of Spades and Three of Spades, that would not have been as good of a magic trick because those cards look so much alike that the audience could get confused about which card is which.

You will also need two more cards. It does not matter what these two cards are because the audience will never see the faces.

You will also need a paper bag and some rubber cement.

The secret to the trick: The two cards that are different from each other, like the Six of Hearts and the Three of Spades, are glued back to back to each other with the rubber cement. Make sure the edges are lined up perfectly so if a person were to look at either side of the card, he or she would not see anything tricky or funny that would make them think there was another card stuck to the back.

Take the other two cards and using the rubber cement, glue them face to face so each side looks like the back of a card.

How to perform the trick: This trick is very easy to perform. Stack the two double-cards that you made, putting the double card with the backs showing on top, and show the paper bag empty. Drop the two cards into the bag.

Tell the audience you made a mistake and forgot to show them the cards. Reach into the bag and take the card that has the faces on each side and take it out, showing one side to your audience. Put it back into the bag, flip it over, and take the card back out, showing the other face.

The audience saw the back of the cards as they went into the bag, then they saw the faces of each card, one at a time. They also saw the bag empty, so no one will think there are more than two cards in the bag.

Each time you do the trick, reach inside the bag, take out the card that has backs on both sides and show it to the audience. Ask someone to guess which card is still in the bag. Reach inside the bag, and as you do, peek at the double face card and make sure when you take the card out of the bag, the side that the volunteer guessed is what is facing the audience, so each time, you are showing that the audience guessed right!

When doing this trick over the internet, using the bag like this helps make sure that no one thinks there are more than two cards.

This trick is also a really good one to do that helps make someone in the audience feel good—by telling your audience that someone is going to guess a card and that they will get it right every time, you are letting your audience know that you are being a nice magician who is going to be very respectful.

I think this is a lot nicer than the way I was taught to do the trick when I was very young. I remember reading about this trick in a book and the instructions told you that whenever your volunteer guessed which card, you were supposed to show the other face of the card, so every time you did the trick, the person helping you out would get it wrong.

I did not want someone who was nice enough to help me to be wrong every time, because I was afraid they would feel bad.

So I started doing the trick the way that you just read about in this chapter. You know what happened? People started liking the trick a lot more!

Trick #3: 3-Card Monte

When I do this trick, I use really big cards and show this to 400-500 kids at a time on a big stage. With this version, you can do it over the internet and because it's on a computer screen, everyone will be able to see it!

What the trick looks like to the audience: Monte The Magician holds three cards in a fan in his left hand. He shows them to the audience. The three cards in the fan are all black cards: the Six of Clubs, Three of Spades, and Four of Spades.

"I have three black cards here, and sometimes I have trouble telling them apart. So when I forget which card I'm holding, I use magic to help me."

Monte turns the faces of the cards in his left hand away from the audience. Using his right hand, he carefully pulls the middle card out, with it's back still facing the audience.

He turns the two remaining cards in his left hand around, showing two of the remaining black Spade cards.

Monte asks, "Do you know which card I took?" Some people in the audience make guesses. Others shake their heads, showing they are not sure either.

Monte says, "You know what? Since I have been talking to you, I don't remember either. So I made it change!"

He turns the single card in his right hand around, showing that the last black card has turned into a bright red Ace of Hearts!

What you need for this trick: You'll need four playing cards. To do the trick like I did, you will need three black cards and one red card, but you can do it with any cards that you like. I will explain why I do the trick the way that I do later in these instructions.

You will also need a pair of safety scissors and some clear Scotch tape.

The secret to the trick: When you show the three black cards in a fan, the center black card is really just a flap, a small corner part of a card. The red card is slid underneath the card flap. Then the last black card is placed over the red card and part of the flap. When the cards are held in a fan, it looks like you are just holding three black cards, even though one of them is a red card.

To make the special flap card, take all three of the black cards and lay them on top of each other and square them up, then make a fan.

When you have your cards laid out in a fan, look at the part of the middle card that is showing. You are going to cut that part of the card, the corner with the number, away from the rest of the card. After you cut the card, you'll have a big corner of the card that has the number showing.

Take a piece of the Scotch tape that is a little shorter than the flap. Stick the tape so half of it is stuck to the face down, or back, side of the flap you cut. Put the flap face down on one of the other black cards. Press the tape in place. Now fold the flap over onto the face of the whole card, so that you can see the number on the corner of the flap card.

Placing the tape and the flap on the card this way means that the Scotch tape is hidden from view of the audience and when you fold the flap card over to see the number, you have created a sort of little pocket where you can slide the red card, face up, right under the flap.

Take the remaining black card and place it so one side overlaps the flap just a little bit.

With everything in place, you can hold up the fan of cards, and it will look like you are holding up a little fan of three black cards and the red card is totally hidden!

I remember the first time I made one of these, it took me a couple of tries to get that little flap taped in the right place, so if it does not look right, peel the tape off and keep trying.

How to perform the trick:

When you perform the trick, hold the fan of cards in your left hand by pinching the bottoms of the cards between your thumb and first finger.

Show everyone the faces of the cards. Then turn your left hand inward by the wrist, so now the audience sees the back of the cards.

With your right hand, pull the middle card, which is really the red card, out from underneath the other cards and flap.

Hold the card in your right hand, with the back of the card facing the audience.

Using your left thumb, slide the two cards in your left hand closer together so that the flap is completely hidden, but you can still see the two corner numbers of the remaining cards.

Then turn your left wrist back toward the audience, showing everyone the two black cards.

Then for the big magic moment, turn your right hand around, showing that card has "magically" changed from a black card to a red card!

The reason I use three black cards and make one of them change to a red card is because the red card is very surprising to see—people see the difference between a black card to a red card right away.

I also use three black numbered cards that all look sort of the same so that I can tell the story about sometimes I forget which card is which. When audiences see card tricks, they sometimes forget which card is which, too.

So when I tell a story saying that I forget which card, my audience does not feel bad when they also forget which black card is which, because the cards all look very similar to each other.

If I forget too, then I'm not making my audience feel bad. When I have seen this card trick performed by other magicians, the magicians sometimes say things like, "Which card is in the middle? No, you got it wrong!"

I didn't like it when magicians performed the trick that way. It seemed like they were trying to make themselves look very clever by showing the audience was wrong. It was one of those things that might make people not want to see anymore magic.

Website:

Ask your parents to go to www.VirtualMagicBook.com and enter their name to get you access to the videos for the tricks in this chapter. It's important to ask your parents to do this for you to stay safe online!

In the next chapter, you're going to learn some fun magic with paper, and how to make a magic tree, a magic star, and more!

Chapter 8:
Paper Magic

One of the tricks in this chapter is an amazing magic trick and the other two create instant art! These will be fun!

Trick #1: Cut & Restored Paper

What the trick looks like to the audience: Nancy The Magnificent holds up a long, thin piece of paper.

Nancy says, "I'm trying really hard to not waste resources. Even if I cut a paper, I try to make it so I can use it again."

Nancy demonstrates by folding the paper in half and using a pair of scissors, cuts the paper just below where she folded it. Then she unfolds the paper, revealing that the two halves of the paper have magically become one!

Nancy folds the paper in half and then once again cuts the paper below the fold with the scissors. Once again, she unfolds the paper, and both halves have once again rejoined to make one whole piece of paper!

"I want to make sure that I do not waste paper, so even if I cut the paper at an angle, it still magically goes back together!" Nancy demonstrates by once again folding the paper in half and this time, using her scissors, cuts the folded paper at a sharp angle.

This time, when she unfolds the paper, the two halves have once again joined to be one whole piece of paper, but instead of the entire paper hanging straight down, the bottom half of the strip of paper is at a sharp angle!

What you need for this trick: You'll need the following things:

- A white piece of 8x11 paper
- A pair of scissors
- Rubber cement
- Baby powder

The secret to the trick: The paper is coated with rubber cement, so every time you cut the paper, the rubber cement keeps the edges of each half sticking together!

To prepare the trick, using the scissors, cut one long strip of paper from the 8x11 piece of paper.

Using the rubber cement, coat most of one side of the strip of paper, leaving only an inch or so of each end uncoated. Let the rubber cement dry for several minutes. Once it's dry, re-coat the same area on the paper again with rubber cement. Let it dry again for several minutes.

Once dry, sprinkle the coated surface of the paper with the baby powder. Before doing this step, make sure you have a newspaper or paper place mat or something on the table to protect the surface and collect the extra baby powder so you can throw it away later.

Shake off the extra baby powder, and now your strip of paper is ready! Using the white baby powder on top of the white paper means that when everything is done, the paper will look normal.

You are ready to perform!

How to perform the trick: To perform the trick, fold the paper in half, with the coated side of the paper on the inside of the fold. Using the scissors, cut through both layers of paper a little below the fold.

Carefully unfold the paper, showing it has been restored. The reason this works is because the baby powder keeps the rest of the paper from sticking to itself. As the scissors cut, the blades cut through the baby powder and force the exposed rubber cement to stick to itself, so the very edges of the paper where it's cut hold the two cut pieces of paper together. It's a perfect illusion!

Because you put rubber cement (and baby powder) along so much of the paper, each time you fold the paper and cut it with scissors, the rubber cement keeps the two halves of paper together...even when cutting the paper at an angle!

You can use any story that you want with this trick. I like using an environmental message about not wasting paper because most of the time when I perform magic, I am using my tricks to give important messages to my audiences.

Trick #2: Newspaper Tree

What the trick looks like to the audience: Oprah The Amazing holds up several sheets of newspaper that have been taped together end to end.

"Instead of just throwing the newspapers my dad reads away, I learned how to make some paper art," she says.

Oprah rolls up the sheets of paper into a tube. Then, using a pair of scissors, she makes four cuts into the paper tube, starting from the top, going down about a third of the way into the tube.

When she finishes cutting, the parts of the tube that she has cut are flopping down, looking sort of like branches to a tree. Reaching into the center of the 'branches,' she gently pulls some of the branches up.

The tube gets longer and longer and the layers of branches spread out more along the length of the rolled tube of paper until it looks like a paper tree, with several branches along the 'trunk' of the tree!

What you need for this trick: You'll need a newspaper, some Scotch tape, and a pair of scissors.

The secret to the trick: This really is not a magic trick but is more of a cool piece of 'paper art.'

Take a newspaper and remove one sheet. If the sheet of newspaper you have is very wide and opens like a book, you will want to tear it in half along the fold where you would open it to read the inside.

Take three or four of those half-sheets and lay them short end to short end and overlap them over each other by a few inches. Tape them together using the Scotch tape. When you finish, you should have one looooong piece of newspaper!

How to perform the trick: To perform the trick, roll up the newspaper into a loose tube. Using your scissors, cut down into the rolled 'tube' of newspaper about one third of the length of the rolled tube, being sure to cut through all of the layers.

Then make another cut right across from the first cut. After the second cut, the layers of newspaper will probably start getting all floppy because when the layers are cut, they are not able to stay straight up and down anymore.

Make another cut down the length of the paper through the center of one of the halves, then make a final cut through the other half.

If that sounds confusing, think of it like this: If you look down on the top of the rolled tube of paper, it's the same shape as a clock. Make your first cut down into the tube where the "12" would be on the clock. Make the second cut at the spot where the "6" would be. Make the third cut where the "9" would be and make the fourth cut where the "3" would be.

As you make each cut, the layers of the paper in the rolled-up tube may get flippy-floppy, so you make need to sort of hold the layers together as you cut. Always be super-careful using scissors!

When you are done cutting, reach your hand inside the tube and begin gently tugging up on some of the inner layers of cut pieces of paper which will form the branches of the tree.

As you tug upward, the paper will want to unroll a little. Keep pulling upward and the tree will get taller and taller, and the branches will spread out more and more, giving you a very cool looking tree!

Trick #3: Star

What the trick looks like to the audience: Preta the Magician tells someone in her audience on Zoom that because she likes them so much, she is going to make a star for them.

"And to make it even harder on me, I am going to make this star with only one cut with my scissors!" she says.

She folds a piece of paper several times and cuts the folded paper into two pieces with a pair of scissors.

Preta unfolds the smaller of the two pieces, revealing it is a perfect star!

What you need for this trick: You'll need one piece of 8x11 paper and one pair of scissors.

The secret to the trick: This is not so much a magic trick as it is kind of like 'paper art,' sort of like the paper tree. This works because the paper is folded several times in a special way and then cut with the scissors at just the right place, leaving you with a perfect star!

How to perform the trick: I myself had to fold and cut over 20 pieces of paper before I finally learned this. This trick can be very challenging to understand from written instructions, but as I mentioned earlier in this book, it's good exercise for your brain, so try it a couple of times with this book and then if you still have trouble, you can easily learn this by having your parents go to the video of me demonstrating this for you.

Here are the step-by-step instructions:

1. Start with a sheet of 8x11 of paper on the table in front of you. Make sure the paper's short end is closest to you.
2. Fold the paper in half, bringing short end that is farthest from you toward the end that is closest to you. Crease the fold.
3. Spin the folded paper one-quarter turn so that once again, the short side of the paper is closest to you. Fold the paper in half again, bringing the short end that is farthest away toward the end that is closest to you and crease your fold again.
4. Unfold the paper completely. You will see the paper has two folds, one horizontal and one vertical. Fold the paper in half once again, right along the same crease you made in step 1.
5. Make sure the paper is resting on the table with the long side of the paper, the folded side, farthest

away from you. The opposite long side of the paper, with open ends of the paper, should be closest to you.

6. Using your left hand, you are going to fold the upper left corner toward the right side of the paper. You are going to put that corner of the paper toward the middle of the right side of the paper...but you are not going to put that corner that you are folding completely at the edge of the right side. Why? Because you are going to use the vertical middle crease in the paper as a guide and stop your folding at that vertical fold line. Crease the fold you just made.

7. Take that same corner (the one that started off at the upper left corner of the paper) and fold that corner back to the left, so those two sides line up. Crease the fold.

8. Looking at what you have now, take the upper right hand corner (you have not done anything else with this corner), and fold it so that entire side of the paper is folded against the crease you made in step 7. Crease that fold.

9. Take that same corner that is now farthest on the left and fold it back so that edge of the paper lines up perfectly with the fold you made in Step 8. Crease that fold. You should have something now that sort of looks like a flattened, pointy paper airplane.

10. Pick up the folded paper. Hold it in your left hand, with the pointy end facing up.

11. Take your scissors in your right hand. You are going to cut the paper, starting off at the point of the top fold along the right side of the paper. Don't cut the paper in half... aim your scissors a little higher, so as you cut through the paper from the right side toward the left, your cut is a straight line that starts from that right corner and ends about two inches from the pointy top of the paper.

12. After the cut, you'll have two pieces of folded paper—a big piece and a little piece. Throw away the biggest piece of paper. Unfold the smaller paper. If everything went well, you should now have a star!

This is probably the hardest trick in the book to explain with written words so if you have trouble, be sure to ask your parents to get access to the videos of me performing and teaching all of the tricks in this book.

Website:

Ask your parents to go to www.VirtualMagicBook.com and enter their name to get you access to the videos for the tricks in this chapter. It's important to ask your parents to do this for you to stay safe online!

Chapter 9:
Sleight of Hand

If you learn some sleight of hand, you can do magic anytime, anywhere! There are thousands of tricks, moves, and routines using basic to advanced sleight of hand. If you are new to magic, these moves will be a nice introduction to using nothing more than normal objects and special moves with your hands to create magic.

Trick #1: Changing Spots

What the trick looks like to the audience: Quinoa The Nifty Magician holds up a six-sided die to his webcam where his audience is watching.

"Have you ever played a game like Monopoly or Life and wished you had rolled a different number? Watch this," he says.

Holding the die between his right finger and thumb, he shows one side of the die. The number on it is six dots. He turns his right wrist over, so his audience can see the other side of the die. The number is four dots.

Quinoa asks, "What number was on the other side?"

The audience responds by saying, "Six." Niles turns his wrist back to where he started, showing the six dots on the die.

"Thanks!" Quinoa says. "What number is on the opposite side?"

The audience says, "Four." Quinoa turns his wrist again, showing the side of the die with four dots on it.

"Thank you! My memory is really bad today. What number is on the other side?" Quinoa asks.

The audience says, "Six." Quinoa turns his wrist again, showing the six dots on that side of the die.

"So that means there is a four on the other side, at least I think..." Quinoa says.

Quinoa slowly turns his wrist one more time. Now the die only has one dot on that side!

What you need for this trick: You'll need one regular six-sided die from any board game like Monopoly or Life.

The secret to the trick: The numbers change because as you are turning your wrist to show the opposite side of the die, you are also, at the same time, moving your right finger and thumb in opposite directions, causing the die to rotate one turn, pivoting on the corner, which causes the die to display a different number on the visible side.

As you turn your wrist back, you reverse the move, allowing the die to go back to its original side.

People often talk about moves in magic being "quicker than the eye," but most of the time it is not true. If you move your hands too quickly, people will think something funny is going on. Moving your hands too quickly actually causes people to look even more closely at whatever you are doing.

What keeps people from noticing that you are turning the die with your fingers is the fact that at the exact same time, you are also turning your wrist, which is a much bigger move.

So, in magic, we can use big physical movements to hide smaller movements that we want to keep hidden.

As with all of the magic in this book, practice doing the secret turn as you turn your wrist while watching yourself in a mirror. For me, I find that doing the secret move when my wrist is about halfway through its turn works well for me, but by watching yourself in a mirror, you will find what works best for you.

How to perform the trick: When you look at a die, the dots on opposite sides always add up to seven. So five and two are on opposite sides, three and four are on opposite sides, and six and one are on opposite sides.

Because of that, I always start the trick by showing the side with six dots. Then as I rotate my wrist, I change the other side from the one (which it should be) to another number.

Seeing another number change to a one shows up really well on a webcam!

I keep doing the secret move each time I turn my wrist so that at the very end of the trick, as I turn my wrist for the last time, I can go reeeeaaaallll slooooooow as I show that the die's side has turned to a one, which is very surprising.

Trick #2: Appearing Coin

This is one of the very first sleight of hand tricks I ever learned! This will take some practice, but it is worth it.

What the trick looks like to the audience: Rocket The Magician says to his audience, "You know, I really wish I had some money. Let me try something."

Rocket shows his left hand empty. He waves his right hand over his left hand, opening and closing it a couple of times, and the last time she opens his left hand, suddenly there is a quarter on the palm of his hand!

What you need for this trick: You'll need only a quarter and your two hands for this trick!

The secret to the trick: The quarter is secretly held in your right hand and as the left hand closes the last time, the right hand secretly drops the quarter into your left hand.

To start the trick, pinch the quarter in your right hand, between your thumb and the side of your hand. Because you can't move your thumb, it's important you don't spread your right fingers far apart from each other because that will only cause people to notice your right thumb is not moving. Keep your fingers nice and relaxed, and they will naturally curl and help make your thumb look normal.

Here's the important thing: As you do the trick, you are going to be staring at your left hand and ignoring your right hand. If you stare at something and pay attention to something, that will help direct the audience to look where you want them to look. This is one of the most important things to do in magic.

So, you show your left hand empty with your palm up where the audience can see it, with your right hand at your side. This trick looks best if people are looking straight down into your hand.

How to perform the trick: Start the trick with the coin hidden in your right hand, pinched between the thumb and the side of your hand. Show your left hand empty.

Bring your right hand, palm down, toward your left hand. Start to close your left hand as your right hand's pinky touches your left hand's fingertips. Finish closing your left hand while at the same time pulling your right hand away.

When you do this correctly, no one can actually see into your left hand as you close it because your right hand is blocking the audience from seeing into your left hand for just a moment.

Here's the thing: It should look like your right hand is just sort of waving above the left hand in sort of an "abracadabra" magical hand wave. It should look like the only thing that matters is the left hand and what it is doing.

Do the same motion once or twice: Bringing your right hand, palm down, up to the left hand. Just as the left hand starts to close, touch your right hand's pinky to the fingertips of your left hand. This is when you release your grip just enough so it doesn't look like your thumb has moved but the pressure releases the coin, which falls into your left palm just as the left fingers continue closing... while covered by the palm down right hand.

Take your right hand away, far away. Let that hand rest at your side. Pause for a moment. Then finally open your left hand, revealing the coin that "magically" appeared there.

Spend a lot of time practicing this in front of a mirror and then recording yourself with a phone or video camera. Everyone's hands and fingers are different. You might want to let go of the coin just a teeny bit sooner than I suggested. Or maybe you want to let go of it a teeny bit later. Practice it and see what looks best for your fingers and hands.

You can also try different sized coins. I suggested using a U.S. quarter, but that is because that size works best for me and my hands. You can try a penny, a dime, a nickel... whatever works best for you.

Have fun, this is a really fun trick!

Trick #3: French Drop Vanish

This sleight of hand move is so important that even Penn & Teller teach it in their class about magic! I learned this trick almost forty years ago, and I still use it almost every time I do magic!

What the trick looks like to the audience: In her left hand, Scarlet is holding the coin that she just made magically appear.

"That looked really cool, but this coin is not real. I was just pretending to have a coin."

As Scarlet says this, she takes the coin in her right hand... and opens her right hand to show that it has vanished!

"But if I really wanted a coin," she says, "I would just take a real one out of my pocket." As she says this, she reaches into her pocket with her left hand and takes a coin out.

What you need for this trick: You'll need the same coin you used for the last trick and your two hands!

The secret to the trick: The left hand holds the coin as the right hand reaches over to take it... but the right hand only pretends to take the coin. The coin stays in the left hand.

To do this move, hold the coin between your left fingers and thumb by the edge of the coin so that your audience can see the face of the coin.

Reach over with your right hand, palm down, with your fingers open, as if the right hand was going to pick up the coin. Your right fingers should be held close together and slightly curled. The right thumb should be slightly curled, too.

Put your right thumb through the opening in your left hand below the coin but above the left palm. Think of it as if your right thumb was going into a hole.

Stop for a moment. If you are doing this correctly, the left hand is still palm up and holding the coin, and the right hand has approached the left, with the right hand palm down and the right fingers blocking the audience's view of the coin. The right thumb is between the coin and the palm of the left hand.

This is the exact spot where your left fingers release your grip on the coin. It will fall into the left-hand palm.

As soon as the coin falls, slowly and naturally continue closing your right fingers and thumb around the space where the coin used to be, acting as though your right hand is now holding the coin. Keep the right fingers sort of loose, as though the coin was in the right hand, taking up some space, so your right fingers could not close all the way.

At the same time that the right hand is closing its fingers, allow your left fingers to curl slightly, and begin to turn your left hand palm down as the right hand pulls away.

By curling the fingers of the left hand, even though the left hand is now palm down, toward the floor, the coin will remain safe and hidden in the left hand.

When you are secretly holding something in one of your hands without anyone knowing that anything is there, it is called "palming." The more natural and less suspicious you can hold your hand, the less people will look at that hand and wonder if you are hiding something.

Do not close your left fingers completely into a fist—your left fingers have to remain partially open so that the audience does not look at your left hand and say, "Hey! I bet it's in your left hand!"

How to perform the trick: Those moves I just described are how to do the trick.

To really make this trick look good, you will need to spend some time using your right hand to actually take the coin away from your left hand. Watch how all of those little motions look when you are really taking the coin.

When you do the secret moves to make the coin disappear, you will want your movements to look as close to the 'real' movements as possible.

After you make the coin disappear, it's a really good idea to make the coin come back only a few seconds later. The longer you wait, the sooner someone might say, "Is it in your other hand?"

In the story above, Scarlet reached into her pocket with her left hand (which was secretly holding the coin) and pretended to take a coin out of her left pocket.

When I do this trick, sometimes I bring my left hand (with the coin still palmed in my left hand) to my nose and make a sneezing sound and pretend I'm sneezing the coin out of my nose!

Website:

Ask your parents to go to www.VirtualMagicBook.com and enter their name to get you access to the videos for the tricks in this chapter. It's important to ask your parents to do this for you to stay safe online!

Chapter 10:
Science Tricks

I love science!

Two of the tricks in this chapter are more of logic puzzles—ways of figuring out a solution to something—and the last trick is truly amazing.

If you enjoy this chapter, be sure to check out my book, *Super Science: Unleash Your Superpowers With These Fun Experiments* for more science fun!

Trick #1: Balloon and Glass Trick

What the trick looks like to the audience: Terri the Great Magician shows her audience a glass of water and asks if anyone can think of a way to lift the glass of water without touching the glass?

Some audience members actually suggest ideas. Terri listens to some of the ideas and compliments them. Then she says she has an idea, too.

"This is really cool," Terri says. "I'm excited to show you this!"

Terri shows an uninflated balloon and rests the body of the balloon in the glass, while holding the neck of the balloon between her fingers. She blows up the balloon large enough to make the balloon airtight inside the glass.

Holding the balloon tightly by the neck so the air does not escape, Terri lifts the balloon up into the air, and the glass of water comes with it!

What you need for this trick: You'll need a glass about half full of water and a round balloon. The balloons I use most often are 9" round balloons.

The secret to the trick: When the balloon is blown up enough to become air tight inside the glass, two things make it possible to lift the glass: The friction of the balloon against the inside of the glass keeps the balloon from slipping out, and the big secret is the air pressure under the balloon but above the water in the glass also holds the balloon in place, allowing you to easily lift the glass with the balloon.

How to perform the trick: This is not so much a magic trick but more of what is sometimes called a "betcha," which means the person doing the trick issues a challenge for something that seems impossible and the person doing it tries to get the people watching to bet against the possibility of success... sometimes even for money!

This trick, like a lot of "betchas," can seem like you are showing off by asking the audience if they can figure something out, and if they can't, you have the solution. Notice in the story, Terri lets other audience members suggest possible solutions and then instead of sounding like a know-it-all with the solution, she says that she is excited to show them how it works.

Sometimes, just having a different attitude is what makes a trick more appealing to people.

Trick #2: Through a Postcard

What the trick looks like to the audience: Ultron the Great holds up a postcard-sized index card to his audience.

"Did you know that there is a way to cut this little index card so that you can actually poke your head through it?"

Ultron then holds the notecard and, using a pair of scissors, makes a series of cuts across the index card. '

He then reveals that the notecard has opened up, with an opening in the center large enough to put his head through!

What you need for this trick: You'll need a notecard. I usually use a 5x7 size, but you can use any size you like. You'll also need a pair of scissors.

The secret to the trick: This trick is accomplished by altering the perimeter (the outline) of the index card so that the hole in the middle of the card will be big enough to fit a person's head through.

Cutting a hole in the middle of the card will not be enough... the card must be cut in a special way. I will explain the instructions thoroughly, and if you need more help, you can watch the video of me doing this.

Here are the steps:

1. Take the index card and fold it exactly in half lengthwise.
2. Hold the folded card with the short ends facing up and down.
3. Using your scissors, cut through the card near the top, right through the fold, but only cut through about three-quarters of the width of the card.
4. Then move your scissors to the opposite side of the fold and start cutting from that side but start

cutting about a quarter of an inch down. Continue cutting about three-quarters through the width again.

5. Move your scissors back to the folded side of the card and start cutting about a quarter of an inch below where the last cut took place.

6. Move your scissors back to the opposite side of the fold, and start cutting from that side, but start cutting about a quarter of an inch down. Continue cutting about three-quarters through the width again.

7. Continue going back and forth and cutting from side to side, but only making your cuts about three-quarters the width of the card, until you have come to the bottom of the card.

8. Next, look at the folded side of the card. Because of the cuts you made, you are going to have several separate folds. You are going to snip off just the folds, but in a special way.

9. Before you do any cutting, count up the number of separate folds on that side of the card. Let's pretend you have ten separate folds. You are going to leave the first and tenth folds (the ones on the ends) alone.

10. Now you are going to cut through the rest of those middle folds.

11. This will allow you to open up the notecard, giving you an opening much larger that allows you to put the card over someone's head!

How to perform the trick: This is another "betcha" kind of trick where the solution is not so much magical as it is interesting. To make the trick seem less like you are trying to fool someone, in this case, I wrote the story in such a way that the magician told his audience right away that there was a solution to the problem.

Again, showing a "betcha" can sometimes seem like the magician is showing off, showing that he or she can do things that no one else can. I think it's much better to show tricks like this as though the magician just wants to share something fun with his or her audience instead of showing off.

This is a way to be kind and respectful to your audience— they will like you and enjoy your performing even more.

Trick #3: Mobius Strip

What the trick looks like to the audience: The Amazing Valkrye holds up a long, thin piece of paper. She tapes the ends together, forming a loop. She cuts down through the middle of the strip of paper, down the entire length, until the loop of paper has been cut into two thinner loops of paper.

"Let's try that again but make it weird!" Valkrye says. She picks up another strip of paper that has already been taped end to end into a loop. She once again cuts right down the middle of the strip of paper... but this time, when she finishes cutting, instead of two separate loops, the paper is one giant loop!

"Would you like to see it again... but even weirder?" Valkrye asks.

Her audience on Zoom says yes!

She picks up one more loop of paper and again cuts right down the middle of the strip of paper. After she has cut all the way through the loop and finished where she started, she reveals that she has ended up with two loops of paper... that are mysteriously linked together!

What you need for this trick: You'll need some thin strips of paper that are about two and a half inches wide and about two feet long. You can either cut and tape regular 8x11 paper to make the loops, or you can do what I did— buy a roll of what is called "calculator tape," which is already the right width, which will make doing the trick a lot easier.

You will also need some clear Scotch tape and a pair of scissors.

The secret to the trick: When you take a long strip of paper, tape the ends together, and cut down the middle of the strip of paper until you come back to where you started, you will get two loops of paper. That's what you would expect.

To get the giant loop of paper, here's what you do: Take another strip of paper and when you tape the ends together, twist of the ends over first. This will cause what is called a "Mobius strip," which is an object which mathematically only has one side!

When you cut this strip down the middle, it will cause you to end up with one giant loop.

Next, take a third strip of paper, and before you tape the ends together, twist one of the ends twice, giving you another Mobius strip. This time, when you cut the strip of paper right down the middle, you will automatically wind up with two separate loops of paper linked together!

How to perform the trick: This trick can be performed as a magic stunt, a science experiment, or even as a fun mystery where the magician does not even know what happened.

<u>Website:</u>

Ask your parents to go to www.VirtualMagicBook.com and enter their name to get you access to the videos for the tricks in this chapter. It's important to ask your parents to do this for you to stay safe online!

Our next chapter is about creating magic where it looks like you are reading minds!

Chapter 11:
Mind Reading Magic

This chapter includes two mind reading methods where your audience does not realize it, but you are actually "forcing" them to pick an item that you want them to select.

In magic, "forcing" something on a person means that you invite a volunteer to pick one thing from a group of items—like a card from a deck of cards, a coin from a pile of coins, or whatever—and the person thinks they can choose whatever they want, but you as the magician controls what happens so the volunteer winds up picking the one thing that you wanted them to pick. Then, because you knew what they would pick far in advance, you can have a prediction showing that you knew in advance what they would pick.

The last trick is a math trick that lets your audience have a free choice in what numbers they select but the end of the trick actually gives your audience the same result every time.

Trick #1: Hot Rod Force

What the trick looks like to the audience: William The Amazing lays out six items and an envelope on a table.

The six items are, from left to right: a pen, a pencil, a quarter, a cup, a rubber band, and a cookie. He asks one person in his audience to say any number from one to six out loud.

The audience member says, "Three."

William starts counting starting from the left, counting three items, landing on the quarter. He picks up the envelope and opens it, showing a piece of paper that reads, "I predict you will pick the quarter."

What you need for this trick: You'll need a piece of paper to write your prediction on, a pen, an envelope, and any small six objects.

Since this book is devoted to tricks you can do over the internet, the six items that you pick should be small enough that you can set them in a single row on your table, and everyone will be able to see them all.

You will also want to be sure that it is easy for your audience to tell all of the objects apart from each other. That means you wouldn't want to use two blue crayons that are slightly different shades!

The secret to the trick: This trick works by having the item you want to have selected in a certain place in line, and when the audience member says a number, you change how you use that number to land on the selected item every time.

Let's go back to the story with William. The six items were, from Uber's left to right: a pen, a pencil, a quarter, a cup, a rubber band, and a cookie.

In the story, the volunteer says the number three, so Uber started counting, starting on his left, from one to three. He automatically landed on the quarter, which is what he had written on a piece of paper.

But here is what William did NOT do: He never told the audience exactly how their number was going to be used! In other words, he did not tell the audience which side of the row of items he was going to start on. He also did not even tell the audience he was going to count at all.

Because he did not say how he was going to use the number the audience member gave him, William was free to start from either side of the row and also free to count or spell, depending what he needed to do.

Here's what William would have done for all of the six different numbers:

If the audience member said "one," William would have started with the pencil (on his left side) and spelled "o-n-e," landing on the quarter.

If the audience member said "two," William would have started with the pencil (on his left side) and spelled "t-w-o," landing on the quarter.

If the audience member said "three," William would have started with the pencil (on his left side) and counted "1...2...3," landing on the quarter.

If the audience member said, "four," William would have started with the cookie (on his right side) and counted "1...2...3...4," landing on the quarter.

If the audience member said, "five," William would have started with the cookie (on his right side) and spelled "f-i-v-e," landing on the quarter.

If the audience member said, "six," William would have started with the pencil (on his left side) and spelled "s-i-x", landing on the quarter.

How to perform the trick: As you can see, this is a very simple trick to perform and you can use any six items that you want. One fun thing to do that will work over the internet is have one of your volunteers pick any six objects and put them in a row. As the audience member is setting everything up, you take out a piece of paper and write down the object they set at the "third from the left, or fourth from the right" position.

Here's the most important thing about performing this trick: You have to practice what you say so that no matter what number your volunteer names, you very quickly say, "Great! We will count to your number," or "Great! We will spell your number."

By practicing what you say over and over before you do the trick, you will be acting and speaking in a very natural way which makes the trick more convincing.

If you don't practice much, after an audience member says a number, you might hesitate as you have to think about whether you need to spell or count. When you speak, you might sound like you are not sure what you need to do and you might say your words like this: "Okay...uh...five...that means...we are going to spell, starting on this side.

With most mind reading magic tricks, there are not very many special sleight of hand moves to do, so your words and how you say them becomes much more important. Unless you practice what you are going to say over and over, the way you speak might accidentally let the audience know that what you are doing is a puzzle, and no one wants to see a puzzle... they want to see magic!

This trick, or I should say, this "force" got its name, the Hot Rod Force, because in some magic websites, you can buy a small plastic magic wand that has six different colored jewels on it.

Let's pretend the colors are, from left to right: blue, yellow, red, green, purple, and yellow.

When someone tells you a number from one to six, you get to their number by spelling or counting to the red jewel because that is the jewel in that "third from the left" position.

Then, you slide the magic wand into the closed fist of your other hand, and when you take it back out, all of the jewels have magically changed to red!

The magic wand has a row of six red jewels on the bottom of the wand, so when you put the wand into your hand, you secretly turn it over, so when you pull the magic wand back out of your fist, it looks like all the jewels changed to red, which was the number "picked."

One other thing I should say about this "force" is that a lot of magicians do not like it because they think that when someone names a number, that you should always count the number and never spell. They think the spelling of the number is silly and no one is fooled by it.

When I do magic, I try not to use this "force," but sometimes, depending on the trick that I am trying to create, it's the only thing that will work.

I feel that if you are new to magic, this is a good "force" to start with. It will give you good practice because you have to practice changing what you say by reacting to whatever choice your volunteer gives you.

The next "force" in this chapter is more deceptive but takes a little more practice to make it look and sound fair and magical.

Trick #2: PATEO Force

What the trick looks like to the audience: Xander the Great invites someone in his audience to line up seven different objects in a line—a penny, a pencil, a book, a stuffed animal, a dollar bill, a comb, and a carrot—so Xander can see all of them on his computer screen.

Xander holds up an envelope.

"I have written something very cool on a piece of paper inside this envelope," Xander explains. I'll show you what it is, but first let's play a game!

"Here's what we are going to do: You are going to point to two of those objects. I will tell you which of those two we are going to get rid of. Then I will point at any two of those objects, and you'll decide which one we are going to get rid of. We will take turns doing that until there is just one object left."

Xander and his volunteer start the game, with the volunteer pointing at the penny and the book, and Victor saying that the penny is eliminated.

Then Xander points at the book and the dollar, and the volunteer eliminates the dollar.

Then the volunteer points at the stuffed animal and the book, and Xander eliminates the book.

Xander points at the stuffed animal and the pencil, and the volunteer eliminates the pencil.

The volunteer points at the comb and the carrot, and Xander eliminates the comb.

The last two items left are the carrot and the stuffed animal.

Xander says, "Okay, there are only two items left. When I count to three, say one of the items out loud. One...two...three!"

The volunteer says "Carrot!"

"Great!" Xander says, "Please set the carrot aside with the other eliminated items. We have the stuffed animal as our choice!"

Xander opens the envelope and pulls out a piece of paper that has THE STUFFED ANIMAL written on it in big letters!

What you need for this trick: The only thing you really need for this trick is a piece of paper to write down the prediction. You don't have to use an envelope like Xander did in the story.

Also, in this story, Xander let his volunteer over the internet pick out several items. If you want to, you can have seven items ready on your own table when you start this trick.

The secret to the trick: This is another "force," but this looks a more mysterious and fair than the Hot Rod Force because the volunteer gets to make choices each time, too.

This force is called the PATEO force. PATEO stands for Pick Any Two, Eliminate One.

The way that it works is simple. Whenever you do the force, you will start by showing your volunteer how it works. You will point to any two of the items on the table that is NOT the item you want to predict.

In the story with Xander, he wanted to force the stuffed animal. If the volunteer pointed at the stuffed animal and one other item, Xander would always choose the other item to be eliminated.

Whenever it was time for Xander to point at two items, he would never point at the stuffed animal so the volunteer would never have a chance to eliminate it.

When Xander got down to the last two items—the stuffed animal and the carrot—and it was the volunteer's turn to pick one item, Xander said, "Okay, in a second, one of these two items is going to become more important to you! On the count of three, say one of these two items out loud," and then he counted.

In this story, the volunteer said "carrot," so Xander asked the volunteer to put the carrot aside with the other eliminated items. Then he opened his envelope and showed his prediction of the stuffed animal was right.

If the volunteer had said "stuffed animal," Xander would have said, "Great! You picked the stuffed animal as the one thing more important to you." Then he would have opened the envelope and shown his prediction of the stuffed animal was right.

This means that when you get down to the last two items, you have to be careful what you say. If you were to say, "Okay, we have two objects left. Whichever one you say out loud, that is the one I predicted," the volunteer might say the wrong object.

With this kind of trick, the way you say things is really important.

So, with the final two items, it's always really good to say, "When I count to three, one of these two items is going to be more important to you. Say one of them out loud."

That way, that wording is kind of vague, which means you might mean one thing, or you might mean another thing. If the person says "carrot," the carrot might be more important to the volunteer because they would want to eliminate it just like the other objects. Or if the volunteer says "stuffed animal," then it might mean the volunteer would think it's more important because it is the last item.

This means that with mind reading magic, if you are careful how you say things, you can change the rules all the time to force people to pick what you want them to pick, and they won't realize you are changing the rules.

How to perform the trick: This trick looks so fair because you can let your volunteer pick all of the items and they don't have to be set up in a certain order or anything like that.

If you let your volunteer pick all of the items, when you see what they have picked, you can write down which item you want to show you predicted. Just write on a piece of paper on your table below your computer screen so your audience can't see what you are writing.

Here's something really important: If your volunteer starts with a list of ODD items, like 5, 7, or 9, then you will want to let your volunteer point at the first two items to start the game. If your volunteer starts with a list of EVEN items, like 6, 8, or 10 objects, then you will want to start by pointing at two items.

Remembering this rule is important so that when you get to the last two items, it is the volunteer who gets to choose one of the last two objects. If you are the one who gets to choose between the last two objects at the end, your audience might not think you are being fair.

This is a really fun way to do a trick where it looks like you are predicting what someone will choose, and there are no sleight of hand moves. You will still want to spend a lot of time practicing what you will be saying so your speech sounds smooth and natural.

Trick #3: 1089 Force

What the trick looks like to the audience: Magician Yaphit asks his audience if they would like to look into the future! Everyone says yes!

Yaphit selects one person to help him. His name is Tony.

"Tony," Yaphit says, "I want to show everyone here the future, except for you! Do me a favor, and turn your back to your computer, okay?"

Tony turns his back to his computer.

"Thanks, Tony! I'll let you know in just a minute when it is okay to turn around," Yaphit says.

Yaphit then holds the number 1089 written in large numbers on a piece of paper to his computer webcam so that everyone can see it. Yaphit holds his finger up to his mouth, indicating that no one show should say anything. He then puts the paper aside.

"Okay, Tony, you can turn back around!"

Tony turns back to facing his computer.

Yaphit asks Tony to write down on a piece of paper any three digit number, as long as each digit is different. "So 421 would be good but 232 would not. And keep it hidden so none of us can see it," he says.

Once Tony has written his number down, Yaphit asks him to write the number again, but reverse the order. "So if you wrote down 321, now you would write down 123," Yaphit says.

When Tony finishes that, Yaphit says, "Now subtract the smaller number from the larger number. So if you have 421 and 124 written down, you would subtract 124 from 421."

After Tony gets his answer, Yaphit asks him to take this new number and write it down but reverse those numbers. "That means, if your answer is 529, you would reverse it to 925. Once you have those two numbers, add them together," Yaphit requests.

Yaphit waits for Tony to finish and asks him for his answer.

"1089," Tony replies. The audience gasps!

"Tony, while your back was to your computer, I showed this piece of paper to the audience," Yaphit says as he once again holds up his piece of paper with 1089 on it!

What you need for this trick: You'll need a piece of paper and a marker or thick crayon to write down the number 1089 in large numbers so everyone watching on the internet can clearly read it.

That's the only thing you need for the trick!

The secret to the trick: This is a fun self-working trick. Once again, "self-working" means there are no secret moves to do. This trick is based on an algorithm, or series of steps that makes the trick work.

If you follow the math steps outlined in the story with Yaphit, this will work every time, as long as your volunteer is good at math and follows instructions carefully.

Here are the steps:

1. Ask your volunteer to think of a 3-digit number. Every digit must be different, so 123 would work, but 212 or 333 would not work.
2. Once your volunteer writes down their number, ask them to reverse it. So if they wrote down the number 123, reversing it would be 321.
3. Tell your volunteer to subtract the smaller number from the larger number. So if your volunteer had 123 and 321 written down, they would subtract 123 from 321.

4. Ask your volunteer to take whatever their answer is and reverse it. For example, subtracting 123 from 321 would give you 198. If they reverse that number, they would have 891.
5. Now your volunteer can add up the last two numbers. 198 plus 891 equals 1089!
6. Once again, if your volunteer does the math correctly, the answer will always be 1089!

How to perform the trick: The real secret to this trick, the one that you need to really practice, is giving the instructions what to do very clearly and carefully. Some people struggle with math, even simple math, so for the trick to work, you have to make sure that your volunteer understands each step before you move on to the next.

If you are reading this and thinking, "This is easy! No one will have trouble with this," then I have a story for you.

I was doing this trick at a middle school in front of 200 7th graders. To make sure the math was correct, I brought up a teacher to help my volunteer to make sure the math was done correctly.

Both the student and teacher did the math incorrectly. Doing math, especially when many people are watching you, can be a little intimidating, even if it's just supposed to be fun for some friends over the internet.

Also, for the performing, Yaphit started off by showing everyone (except for Tony) the prediction! Because this math trick has the same answer every time (when the math is done correctly) then showing your audience the prediction right at the beginning of the trick is something fun you can do.

Most of the time when I do this trick, I put the paper that says 1089 on it into an envelope and show the envelope before the trick starts, so my audience knows that I have a prediction, but they don't know what it says until the end of the trick.

I think you can do it either way, and I included the story of Yaphit doing it the way he did to show you a trick can be done many different ways.

Have fun with this trick, make sure you explain the steps very carefully, and get ready to amaze some friends!

Website:

Ask your parents to go to www.VirtualMagicBook.com and enter their name to get you access to the videos for the tricks in this chapter. It's important to ask your parents to do this for you to stay safe online!

Chapter 12:
Conclusion

We have reached the end of this book, and it's one that I have really enjoyed writing! I did some research on the internet, and I have not seen any other books devoted completely to performing magic over the internet for kids, so I'm proud of being the first one, and if it turns out I'm not the first, I'm at least early in the game!

Remember, I encourage and challenge you to read this book thoroughly and try your best to do the tricks based on what I have written. Learning information like this is really good exercise for your brain!

Since magic requires a lot of practice to look really amazing, you'll need to re-read this book many times. As you go through the book a second time, notice a few things:

☺ With every trick, the idea is not to "fool" people. The main idea is to entertain people and help them have a good time!

☺ Nearly every trick had a little story, even if it was short. Having a story or some kind of presentation will always make magic more interesting to people

☺ Even though this book is about performing magic over the internet, I tried to get people involved for every trick by doing different things, like asking questions, getting everyone to count, asking people to do things like write numbers, and so on.

☺ I tried to stress over and over the ideas of being respectful and kind throughout the book. Not only will doing this make you a better magician, but it will help you in so many ways in life!

Remember, if you need extra help with these tricks, you can always ask your mom or dad to go to the website www.VirtualMagicBook.com to get FREE access to the videos of me performing and teaching every trick in this book!

While this is the end of my first book on virtual magic for kids, it definitely does not need to be the end for you in the world of magic! There are thousands upon thousands of books written about magic. Many of those tricks can be used to perform magic over the internet.

Also, I have other books I have published, including *Super Science: Unleash Your Superpowers With These Fun Experiments,* and many more on the way, including another magic book that will be titled *Gross Magic*! If you enjoyed this book, ask your parents to go to the website www.VirtualMagicBook.com and fill in their information. Then I will send them updates about my other books!

Thank you very much for reading this book!

BONUS Chapter for Parents

Thank you for reading this bonus chapter of *Virtual Magic*. This book has been so much fun to write, mostly because I went into this project with the goal of writing a unique book on magic.

As a child growing up, magic was something that captivated me at a young age, and continued to do so all through high school and college, deep into my late twenties when I finally decided to take the plunge and turn what had been regarded by my parents and most of my friends as a weird little hobby into a full-fledged career.

When people meet me for the first time, they are often surprised that performing magic is my full-time job. Because of this, people of all ages often ask me, "Is there a school that you can go to in order to learn magic?" Yes there is! I'll come back to this a little later.

After being a full-time magician for nearly two decades at the time of this writing, and earning a very good living doing it, I have realized a few things that I think are valuable to keep in mind for kids learning magic, things that I tried to infuse into the fabric of this book, both overtly and covertly.

First, learning magic effectively can help a child increase his or her confidence. When they work to learn something new and they accomplish this, it is a huge boost to a child's self-esteem.

Secondly, when they learn a fun skill like magic that draws people in, it gives the child positive reinforcement. They are receiving the good kind of attention that kids crave.

Third, learning magic can increase eye/hand coordination. For a child in their physical developmental years, this is crucial.

Fourth, magic can stimulate social interaction. For a shy kid like me growing up, the desire to show people fun magic served as a strong motivator to step outside my comfort zone helped me tremendously.

Fifth, when taught properly, magic can help children learn aspects of character education: The value of respecting others and treating others how they want to be treated.

There are literally thousands of books on magic, and many of them are aimed at kids. Most of the ones I have read, especially those aimed at kids, suffer from two major flaws, at least in my opinion.

First, the books focus only on the trick and the secrets to the tricks. Without at least a minimal amount of attention devoted to stagecraft. Even at a young age, magic can turn into a puzzle, and even the most supportive family member can grow weary of magic tricks performed by their sister/brother/son/daughter/niece/nephew.

Second, these books use the idea of 'fooling someone' as the prime motivator for performing magic. After having performed somewhere around 6000 paid performances in my career, I know that almost no one likes to be fooled.

People like to be entertained. They enjoy being entranced.

But being fooled? No way.

The attitude of "I can do something that you can't" in magic, whether overtly stated or not, can cause many people to wrinkle their noses in disdain when magic is mentioned.

For a hobby like magic, which has so much potential to help children positively in their development, there are precious few resources out there to harness these qualities.

So my goal with this book was twofold: First, offer something unique in the world of magic books for kids by focusing all of the tricks on performing over the internet, and secondly, weave throughout this book aspects of good character for kids, such as being respectful of others' interests, listening to what others have to say, good eye contact, being prepared, perseverance, and more.

The first few chapters of this book really drive these important points home, but this theme continues throughout the book, weaving these elements in with the tricks, performance descriptions, explanations, and more. If you happen to be very studied in magic, you'll notice that I slightly reworked some classics of magic to make these character education points even more prominent when possible.

These aspects of character education and social interaction is why I love performing magic for kids. Truthfully, most of my performing involves performing educational assembly programs at schools. In these shows, every trick has an educational message to get across, so the magic becomes a metaphor for a message and a way to remember the messages as well.

Because I feel that magic can offer so much more to children above and beyond just fooling people, I have opened my own online magic school! It's called the Buffalo

Magic Academy, and in addition to teaching kids magic, I like telling parents that it is really a life skills course disguised as a magic class!

My Academy uses the internationally recognized Discover Magic curriculum which has as its goal to teach kids critical aspects of confidence and social skills along with fun magic.

Kids who enroll receive a big box of special high-quality magic props that were custom-created just for this curriculum! They receive a graduation certificate, graduation colored wand (there are four separate courses—Green Wand, Blue Wand, Orange Wand, and Purple Wand), access to hundreds of high-quality online videos, and more.

The best part? I interact directly with your child online, teaching him or her how to do these fun magic tricks while also infusing each online lesson with the character traits so necessary to social development: being respectful, prepared, and many more.

Visit www.BuffaloMagicAcademy.com for more details.

The world of magic has done amazing things for my life, and I hope you and your child decide to explore this wonderful world further!

Once again, thank you for reading this bonus chapter, and I wish you and your child success, both in magic as well as everything you strive to accomplish!

If you have any questions about this book or anything else I offer, please email me at cris@elementaryschoolassemblies.com.

I look forward to hearing from you!

Warmly,

Cris Johnson

See Cris Johnson LIVE!

Cris Johnson offers educational school assembly programs for students in select states across the United States and motivational programs for school faculty!

Visit www.ElementarySchoolAssemblies.com for dates of availability and program information.

Made in the USA
Coppell, TX
08 November 2020

40995836R00114